The Heart of
True Spirituality

JOHN WESLEY'S
OWN CHOICE
Volume 2

The Heart of
True Spirituality

Selections from

THOMAS à KEMPIS, PIERRE POIRET,
JEAN DUVERGIER DE HAURANNE,
and JACQUES JOSEPH DUGUET

FRANCIS ASBURY PRESS
of Zondervan Publishing House

Grand Rapids, Michigan

THE HEART OF TRUE SPIRITUALITY
JOHN WESLEY'S OWN CHOICE: VOLUME 2
Copyright © 1985 by The Zondervan Corporation
Grand Rapids, Michigan

FRANCIS ASBURY PRESS is an imprint of
Zondervan Publishing House
1415 Lake Drive S.E.
Grand Rapids, Michigan 49506

Library of Congress Cataloging in Publication Data

The Heart of true spirituality.

Includes indexes.
Contents: v. 1. Selections from William Law —
v. 2. Selections from Thomas à Kempis (The Christian's
pattern), Pierre Poiret (Instructions for children), Jean Duvergier de
Hauranne (Christian instructions), Jacques Joseph Duguet (Letters on
morality and piety)
1. Devotional literature – Early works to 1800.
2. Christian life – Early works to 1800.   3. Wesley, John,
1703 – 1791.   I. Baker, Frank, 1910 –   .   II. Title: John
Wesley's own choice.

BV4801.H39   1985   248   85 – 13331

ISBN   0 – 310 – 39621 – 2 (v. 1)

Designed and edited by Joseph D. Allison

Printed in the United States of America

85   86   87   88   89   90   /   9   8   7   6   5   4   3   2   1

To
JOSEPH D. QUILLIAN
The Chairman of the Wesley Board

CONTENTS

AN EXPLANATORY
STATEMENT

Even during the lifetime of John Wesley, he and others were making selections from his writings. The most formidable was a three-hundred-page volume published in 1783, entitled *The Beauties of Methodism, selected from the Works of the Reverend John Wesley*. About sixty collections of Wesley's writings are listed in my *Union Catalogue of the Publications of John and Charles Wesley* (1966), pp. 213~19, and some of these passed through many editions. Yet no work thus far has utilized John Wesley's own declared choice of the more significant passages in his publications.

To his method of indicating such selections Wesley referred on several occasions. He began the practice in his editions of Milton's *Paradise Lost* (1763) and Edward Young's *Night Thoughts* (1770), by placing an asterisk before "those passages which I apprehend to be peculiarly excellent, either with regard to sentiment or expression." This method he extended to the thirty-two-volume edition of his own *Works* (1771~74), writing, "The same thing I have taken the liberty to do throughout the ensuing volumes," placing a mark "before those passages which I judge . . . most worthy of the reader's notice." The principal consideration here was spiritual helpfulness rather than literary excellence, though the latter criterion was also important in his selections from Milton and Young.

When these asterisked selections are gathered together into a continuous document it happens frequently~not always~that they possess a unity of their own, presenting in a series of highlights an outline of the general plan of the work, a kind of condensed book. This was apparently a spontaneous continuation of Wesley's method of study at Oxford, where he constantly prepared summaries of books which he read, punctuated by selected illustrative passages. Wesley termed this process "collecting."

Gathering together Wesley's own selections has value quite apart from the synopses which they may offer and the intrinsic worth of the chosen passages themselves. These highlighted documents also furnish a key to Wesley's mind in maturity. They isolate what he considered in his late sixties to be the more important and spiritually helpful passages both in his own writings and in his revised editions of the writings of others (the latter comprising an aggregate of fourteen of the thirty-two volumes of his *Works*). Among these edited works were many spiritual classics which had proved of great importance in his own religious development and pastoral ministry. Such were Thomas à Kempis's *Christian's Pattern*, William Law's *Christian Perfection* and *Serious Call*, two works by John Norris of Bemerton, and four by Jonathan Edwards on the New England revival. This means that we are able to sample the essence of many books which exercised a great influence upon Wesley and which remained significant throughout much of his life.

Each volume is supported by editorial introductions, additional connective material, explanatory extracts, with occasional comments and notes (the latter three categories within square brackets to show that they are not part of Wesley's original emphasized text), and an appendix listing the sources used both by Wesley in editing his originals and by this editor in transcribing Wesley's selections. The text presented is that of the 1771~74 *Works* (in which almost alone these indications of Wesley's choice occur), rather than that of the new Oxford/ Bicentennial edition of his *Works* now in progress, from which on many occasions it differs considerably and which in general does not include most of these edited writings.

Wesley usually placed his asterisks at the beginning of a paragraph, but sometimes in the middle. Each is here represented by a number placed either at the beginning of the selection itself or (where present) of any bracketed introductory matter. In most instances Wesley apparently intended the asterisk to apply to the remainder of the one paragraph only. Occasionally, as when it preceded a simple announcement of the following text (see Law's *Serious Call*, sections 69, 70, and 71) he clearly intended one asterisk to refer to a series of paragraphs, though how many remains uncertain. In these cases all the relevant paragraphs are presented to the end of Wesley's own numbered section; if there is any doubt, the additional paragraphs are treated like other editorial insertions and enclosed within square brackets. A continuous series of paragraphs, each prefixed by an asterisk, is designated by a corresponding series of numbers. In editorial insertions within Wesley's text, ellipses [. . .] are sometimes used to preserve the substance while reducing the length.

In order that Wesley's message should come through with the least hindrance to the reader consistent with the accuracy of the text, various editorial principles have been adopted similar to those in the Oxford/Bicentennial edition of Wesley's *Works*. No words have been added, omitted, or changed in form (except that spelling has been standardized), and the profuse italics found in some works have been removed unless they indicate a major emphasis. Obvious errors have been corrected silently from other editions of Wesley or other authors, but undocumented editorial alterations have been inserted within square brackets.

Frank Baker

Selections from

Thomas à Kempis

DIRECTIONS

How to Read This and Other Religious Books
with Benefit and Improvement

§1. As it is impossible for anyone to know the usefulness of this treatise till he has read it in such a manner as it deserves, instead of heaping up commendations of it, which those who have so read it do not want, and those who have not will not believe, I have transcribed a few plain directions how to read this (or indeed any other religious book) with improvement.

§2. Assign some stated time every day for this pious employment. If any indispensable business unexpectedly robs you of your hour of retirement, take the next hour for it. When such large portions of each day are so willingly bestowed on bodily refreshments, can you scruple allotting some little time daily for the improvement of your immortal soul?

§3. Prepare yourself for reading by purity of intention, whereby you singly aim at your soul's benefit; and then, in a short ejaculation, beg God's grace to enlighten your understanding, and dispose your heart for receiving what you read; and that you may both know what he requires of you, and seriously resolve to execute his will when known.

§4. Be sure to read not cursorily and hastily, but leisurely, seriously, and with great attention, with proper intervals and pauses, that you may allow time for the enlightenings of divine grace. Stop every now and then to recollect what you have read, and consider how to reduce it to practice. Further, let your reading be continued and regular, not rambling and desultory. It shows a vitiated palate to taste of many dishes without fixing upon or being satisfied with any; not but that it will be of great service to read over and over those passages which more nearly concern yourself, and more closely affect your own practice or inclinations, especially if you add a particular examination upon each.

§5. Labour for a temper correspondent to what you read; otherwise it will prove empty and unprofitable, while it only enlightens your understanding without influencing your will, or inflaming your affections. Therefore intersperse here and there pious aspirations to God, and petitions for his grace. Select also any remarkable sayings or advices, treasuring them up in your memory to ruminate and consider on; which you may either in time of need draw forth as arrows from a quiver against temptation, against this or that vice which you are more particularly addicted to; or make use of as incitements to humility, patience, the love of God, or any other virtue.

§6. Conclude all with a short ejaculation to God that he would preserve and prosper this good seed sown in your heart, that it may bring forth its fruit in due season. And think not this will take up too much of your time, for you can never bestow it to so good advantage.

INTRODUCTION TO

The Christian's Pattern

A reading of *De Imitatione Christi*~"Of the Imitation of Christ"~formed one of the major events in the year of John Wesley's ordination, 1725, when he was twenty-two. "I began," he wrote, "to see that true religion was seated in the heart, and that God's law extended to all our thoughts, as well as words and actions" (*Journal*, May 24, 1738, sect. 4). Quoting Kempis himself, Wesley discovered "that 'simplicity of intention and purity of affection' . . . are indeed 'the wings of the soul,' without which she can never ascend to the mount of God" (*A Plain Account of Christian Perfection*, 1766, sect. 3; cf. sects. 86~87 below). He seems first to have read the work in the English translation by Dean George Stanhope, entitled *The Christian's Pattern*, but he soon turned to several of the early Latin versions which had developed from the work of the Dutch Roman Catholic monk, Thomas Hemerken (1380~1471), better known to posterity as Thomas à Kempis. First appearing in print in 1471, this work has been translated into fifty languages and passed through two thousand editions~to which John Wesley himself contributed at least one hundred and twenty editions in four different forms, which have continued to appear even in this century.

Even though Wesley was "very angry at Kempis for being too strict" (*Journal*, May 24, 1738, sect. 4), the *Imitatione* came to mean much to his own devotional life, and to that of the Oxford Methodists for whom he was the spiritual director, so that in 1735 he decided to prepare his own translation. For this he took as his English model an anonymous 1677 translation by Dr. John Worthington (1618~71), with the title *The Christian's Pattern*. This he revised extensively, also using several Latin editions so that the final result was more literal yet more up-to-date, closer to the language of the man in the street. He added a twenty-five-page preface. As a companion to this standard octavo edition illustrated with engraved plates, Wesley also issued the work in a pocket edition.

After his return from Georgia and his own deepened experience of salvation by faith on May 24, 1738~which quickly led to the rapid growth of the new Methodist societies~Wesley published an abridgment of Kempis to enhance their devotional life. He was convinced that the continued pursuit of personal holiness remained essential as an expression of saving faith, and that this classic of Roman Catholic piety would be of even greater value to his Methodist followers if it could be made available to them in a shorter and less expensive form. In 1741, therefore, he published *An Extract of The Christian's Pattern*, reduced to two-thirds of its original length and printed in smaller type on a smaller page. He eliminated the preface and most of the references to practices among religious orders, though he did not attempt to disguise its spiritual origins. He published a Latin edition for translation into English (as an academic exercise) by the scholars at his Kingswood School. He also published an abridgment of book 4 as a preparation for the Lord's Supper, entitled *A Companion for the Altar*. Wesley's varied forms of the work probably added at least a quarter of a million copies to the other millions that have circulated during the last five hundred years.

Throughout the last sixty-five years of his life, this was one of the books that Wesley carried with him as a close companion to his Bible, one which he frequently quoted in his sermons, letters, and devotional writings. There was at least one recorded instance, indeed, when he employed it (as during his earlier years he had regularly employed his Bible) in bibliomancy, opening it at random in order to seek God's guidance about some special problem that could not be solved by reason and prayer alone (*Journal*, April 19, 1764).

So clearly had Wesley made *The Christian's Pattern* his own, that when he came to publish the collected edition of his publications during the years 1771~74, he included in volumes 7 and 8 his *Extract of The Christian's Pattern* ~ once more revised. One of the interesting features of this last revision was his deliberate attempt to remove any amorous expressions, about which he seems to have become even more fastidious in his later years. Thus in section 264, "sweet and" was removed from "good Jesus, sweet and gracious Lord," and in section 268, "O most sweet and loving Lord" became simply "O most loving Lord." Wesley was not consistent in this, however, and in section 192 he retained a similar phrase, "O most sweet and loving Jesus."

As in the other volumes of his *Works*, Wesley distinguished the more significant passages~268 of them, mostly quite brief~with asterisks, implying that he himself had received challenge and support from them: "He rideth easily enough whom the grace of God carrieth" (sect. 112); "If thou bear the cross willingly, it will bear thee" (sect. 131); "Use temporal things, desire eternal" (sect. 183); "Let this be thy prayer . . . , that being stripped of all selfishness, thou mayst follow naked the naked Jesus, and dying to thyself, mayst live eternally with me" (sect. 223). Not that all the memorable passages which Wesley quoted from Kempis were included in this selection, however, as for instance: "*Noli duriter cum tentato*~deal not harshly with one that is tempted" (*Journal*, May 5, 1749, from I.xiii.4); and "Be not familiar with any woman; but in general commend all good women to God" (in a letter to Thomas Roberts, February 12, 1789, quoting I.viii.1 from memory, Wesley wrote, "Remember the wise direction of Kempis, 'Avoid all *good women*, and commend them to God'").

Yet here we have a selection that was undoubtedly special to Wesley, one which he believed might well become special to his followers. Perhaps this might even become true of some of those followers living 250 years after his first publication of the work, in an age when only a fraction of those who honor his courageous and imaginative dedication to God's purposes feel naturally and normally attracted to this soul-searing piety, with its mortifying religious exercises. It is obviously an error to assume that John Wesley's religion was cast in the same mold as our own; likewise it is fruitless to imagine that ours~in a completely different setting~can possibly be cast exactly in his. Nevertheless, whether these meditations make an immediate and positive impact upon us or not, if we are truly to evaluate his lasting influence and message, it is necessary for us to make an imaginative effort to visualize, to understand, and if possible to empathize with his spiritual background. An important ingredient in that background is readily available in John Wesley's own selections from *The Christian's Pattern*.

It should be understood, of course, that Wesley himself did

not mark these passages with the design that they should become a separate devotional manual, but as an aid to those whose taste was not as fully formed as his, and whose attention too easily flagged. After all, these selections contain only one-sixth of even the reduced *Extract*. (Perhaps here there is some proportionate representation between his own protracted devotions and those of his less devout followers, both then and now!) Nevertheless, whatever the reason, these marked meditations do retain a sequence and unity of their own. This I have taken the liberty to augment in two ways: (a) by removing occasional introductory words that do not fit the present context, such as *for* (sect. 36), *therefore* (sect. 115), *yet* (sect. 124), and *who* (sect. 224); (b) by adding within square brackets (as in other volumes in this series), passages that furnish an explanatory context.

From one of the two Latin editions of the *Imitatione Christi* published in Cologne in 1682, Wesley also translated an anonymous "Advice to the Reader." This he first published as an appendix to another early publication of his own, the extract from John Norris's *Treatise on Christian Prudence* (1734). Then it appeared as part 4 of the preface to the octavo edition of his 1735 *Christian's Pattern*, and after that (slightly altered), as the sole preface to his pocket edition of Kempis that same year. This I have prefixed complete to Wesley's selections, as revealing his concern and specific advice about devotional reading, advice equally appropriate both for the large volume in the early eighteenth century and for this small one in the late twentieth century.

THE CHRISTIAN'S PATTERN
BOOK I

*Of the Imitation of Christ, and Contempt
of all the Vanities of the World*

§1. Vanity of vanities! All is vanity but to love God, and to serve him only.

§2. All men naturally desire to know; but what availeth knowledge without the fear of God?

§3. The more thou knowest, and the better thou understandest, the more grievously shalt thou be judged, unless thy life be the more holy.

§4. If thou wilt know anything profitable, love to be unknown, and of no account.

§5. We are all frail, but remember, none more frail than thyself.

§6. He to whom all things are one, who reduceth all things to one, and seeth all things in one, may be stable in heart, and remain peaceable in God.

§7. O God, the truth, make me one with thee in everlasting love!

§8. Let all creatures be silent in thy sight; speak thou alone unto me.

§9. A pure, simple, and stable spirit is not dissipated, though it be employed in many works; because it does all to the glory of God, and seeks not itself in anything it doth.

§10. Surely at the day of judgment we shall not be examined on what we have read, but what we have done; not how well we have spoken, but how religiously we have lived.

§11. Tell me, where are now all those doctors and masters with whom thou wast well acquainted whilst they lived and flourished in learning?

§12. He is truly great that is great in love.

§13. He is truly wise that accounteth all earthly things as dung that he may win Christ.

§14. And he is truly learned that doth the will of God, and forsaketh his own will.

§15. A good life maketh a man wise according to God, and giveth him experience in many things.

§16. All Scripture is to be read by the same Spirit wherewith it was written.

§17. Search not who spake this, but mark what is spoken.

§18. Do what lieth in thy power, and God will assist thy good will.

§19. Trust not in thine own knowledge, nor in any living creature; but rather in the grace of God, who helpeth the humble, and humbleth the poor.

§20. The humble enjoy continual peace; but in the heart of the proud is envy and frequent indignation.

§21. Why are we so fond of conversation, when notwithstanding we seldom return to silence without hurt of conscience?

§22. We willingly talk of those things which we most love or desire, or of those which we feel most contrary and troublesome unto us.

§23. We might enjoy much peace if we would not busy ourselves with the words and deeds of others in which we have no concern.

§24. [If we would endeavour . . . to stand in the battle, we should surely feel the assistance of God from heaven.] For he furnishes us with occasions of striving, that we may conquer.

§25. Wherefore a man should settle himself so fully in God that he need not seek comforts of men.

§26. There is no place so secret where there are no temptations.

§27. When one temptation goeth away, another cometh, and we shall ever have something to suffer.

§28. By patience (through God's help) thou shalt more easily overcome than by harsh and disquieting efforts in thy own strength.

§29. The beginning of temptation is inconstancy of mind, and little confidence in God.

§30. For as a ship without a rudder is tossed to and fro with the waves, so the man that is negligent is many ways tempted.

§31. We know not often what we are able to do, but temptations show us what we are.

§32. We must be watchful, especially in the beginning of the temptation; for the enemy is then more easily overcome if he be not suffered to enter the door of your hearts, but be resisted without the gate at his first knock.

§33. First there occurreth to the mind a simple evil thought; then a strong imagination; afterwards delight; and lastly consent.

§34. Some suffer the greatest temptation in the beginning of their conversion, others in the latter end.

§35. Others again are much troubled almost throughout their life.

§36. God weigheth more with how much love one worketh than how much he doth.

§37. He doth much that loveth much.

§38. [Those things that a man cannot amend in himself, or in others, he ought to suffer patiently, until God order things otherwise.]

Think, that perhaps it is better so for thy trial and patience.

§39. If one that is once or twice warned will not give over, contend not with him; but commit all to God, that his will may be done, and his name honoured in all his servants who well knoweth how to turn evil into good.

§40. If thou canst not make thyself such a one as thou wouldest, how canst thou expect to have another in all things to thy liking?

§41. But now God hath thus ordered it that we may learn to bear one another's burdens; for no man is without fault, no man but hath his burden, no man is self-sufficient, no man has wisdom enough for himself; but we ought to bear with one another, comfort, help, instruct, and admonish one another.

§42. Occasions of adversity best discover how great virtue each one hath.

§43. For occasions make not a man frail, but show what he is.

§44. Help me, O Lord God, in thy holy service, and grant that I may now this day begin perfectly; for that which I have done hitherto is nothing.

§45. Man doth propose, but God doth dispose; neither is the way of a man in himself.

§46. Be thou at no time idle altogether, but either reading, or writing, or praying, or meditating, or endeavouring something for the public good.

§47. One said, As often as I have been among men, I returned less a man; and this we often find true when we have been long in company.

§48. No man safely commands but he that hath learned readily to obey.

§49. And yet the security of the saints was always full of the fear of God.

§50. [Those have often through confidence in themselves fallen into the greatest dangers, who have been in the greatest esteem among men.]

Wherefore it is more profitable to many not to be altogether free from temptations, lest they should be too secure, lest they should be puffed up with pride, or too freely incline to worldly comforts.

§51. O how good a conscience would he keep that would never seek after transitory joy, nor entangle himself with the things of this world!

§52. Leave vain things to the vain, but be thou intent upon those things which God commandeth thee.

§53. It is often better and safer that a man hath not many consolations in this life, especially worldly ones. But that we have not at all or seldom divine consolations is our own fault, because we do not altogether forsake vain comforts.

§54. Miserable thou art wheresoever thou be, or whithersoever thou turnest, unless thou turn thyself to God.

§55. Who is in the best case? He who can suffer something for God.

§56. Arise, begin this instant, and say, Now is the time to be doing, now is the time to be striving, now is the time to amend.

§57. Thou shouldst so order thyself in all thy thoughts and all thy actions as if thou wert to die today.

§58. O that we had spent but one day well in this world!

§59. How wise and happy is he that laboureth to be such in his life as he would wish to be found at the hour of his death.

§60. Whilst thou art in health thou mayst do much good; but when thou art sick, I know not what thou wilt be able to do.

§61. Few by sickness grow better; and they who travel much are seldom sanctified.

§62. Trust not in friends and kindred, neither put off the care of thy soul till hereafter; for men will sooner forget thee than thou art aware of.

§63. But alas! that thou shouldst spend thy time no better here, where thou mightest purchase life eternal. The time will come when thou shalt desire one day or hour to amend in, and I cannot say that it will be granted thee.

§64. Who shall remember thee when thou art dead? Do, do now, my beloved, whatsoever thou art able to do: for thou knowest not when thou shalt die, nor yet what shall be after thy death.

§65. Keep thy heart free, and lifted up to God, because thou hast here no abiding city.

§66. Send thither thy daily prayers and sighs and tears, that after death thy spirit may happily pass to the Lord. *Amen.*

§67. In what thing a man hath sinned, in the same shall he be punished.

§68. When one that was in great anxiety of mind, often wavering between fear and hope, once humbly prostrated himself in prayer, and said, Oh, if I knew that I should persevere! He presently heard within him an answer from God, which said, If thou didst know it, what wouldst thou do? Do what thou wouldst do then, and thou shalt be safe.

§69. Oh, if Jesus crucified would come into our hearts, how quickly and fully should we be instructed in all truth!

BOOK II

Of the Inward Life

§70. Men are soon changed, and quickly fail, but Christ remaineth for ever, and is with us even unto the end.

§71. They that today take thy part, tomorrow may be against thee, and so on the contrary; they often turn like the wind.

§72. Put thy whole trust in God, let him be thy fear and thy love. He will answer for thee, and do in all things what is best.

§73. Why dost thou here gaze about, since this is not the place of thy rest? In heaven ought to be thy dwelling, and all earthly things are to be looked upon as they forward thy journey thither.

§74. All things pass away, and thou together with them.

§75. Beware thou cleave not unto them, lest thou be entangled, and perish.

§76. Christ chose to suffer and be despised; and darest thou complain of anything?

§77. If thou wilt suffer nothing, how wilt thou be the friend of Christ?

§78. If thou hadst but once entered into Jesus, then wouldst thou not be careful about thine own advantage or disadvantage, but wouldst rather rejoice at slanders cast upon thee; for the love of Jesus maketh a man despise himself.

§79. An interior man soon recollecteth himself, because he is never wholly intent upon outward things.

§80. So much is a man hindered and distracted, by how much he cleaveth to outward things.

§81. Nothing so defileth and entangleth the heart of man as the impure love of creatures.

§82. Do not think that thou hast profited anything, unless thou esteem thyself inferior to all.

§83. First therefore have a careful zeal over thyself, and then show thyself zealous for thy neighbour's good.

§84. Our whole peace in this life consisteth rather in humble *suffering* than in not feeling adversities.

§85. He that knows best how to suffer will best keep himself in peace. He is a conqueror of himself, a lord of the world, a friend of Christ, and an heir of heaven.

§86. Simplicity and purity are the two wings by which a man is lifted up above all earthly things.

§87. Simplicity is in the intention, purity in the affection; simplicity tends to God, purity apprehends and tastes him.

§88. No good action will hinder thee if thou be inwardly free from inordinate affection.

§89. If thy heart were right, then every creature would be a looking-glass of life, and a book of holy doctrine.

§90. As iron put into the fire loseth its rust, and becometh all bright like fire, so he that wholly turneth himself unto God is purified from all slothfulness, and is changed into the likeness of God.

§91. He that diligently attendeth unto himself, easily holds his peace concerning others.

§92. Let nothing be great, nothing high, nothing pleasing to thee, but only God himself, or that which is of God.

§93. Esteem all comfort vain which proceedeth from any creature.

§94. A soul that loveth God despiseth all things but God.

§95. God alone, who is everlasting, immense, filling all things, is the comfort of the soul, and the true joy of the heart.

§96. He enjoyeth great peace of mind that careth neither for the praise nor dispraise of men.

§97. What thou art, thou art; neither canst thou be said to be greater than thou art in the sight of God.

§98. To walk inwardly with God, and not to love anything without, is the state of a spiritual man.

§99. He that cleaveth unto a creature shall fall when it falls; he that embraceth Jesus shall stand firmly for ever.

§100. Thou must one day be left of all, whether thou wilt or no.

§101. Whatsoever affection thou reposest in men out of Jesus is all no better than lost.

§102. Trust not, nor lean upon a broken reed; for all flesh is grass, and all the glory thereof shall wither away.

§103. If thou seekest thyself, thou shalt also find thyself, but to thy own destruction.

§104. When Jesus is present, all is well; but when Jesus is absent, everything is hard.

§105. [How dry and cold art thou without Jesus! . . .]

Is not this a greater loss than if thou shouldst lose the whole world?

§106. He is most poor that liveth without Jesus; and he is most rich that is well with Jesus.

§107. Without a friend thou canst not live well; and if Jesus be not above all friends unto thee, thou shalt be very sorrowful and desolate.

§108. Love all for Jesus, but Jesus for himself.

§109. Never desire to be commended or beloved, for that appertaineth unto God.

§110. Neither do thou desire that the heart of any should be set on thee, nor do thou set thy heart on any; but let Jesus be in thee, and in every good man.

§111. Be pure and free within, and entangle not thy heart with any creature.

§112. He rideth easily enough whom the grace of God carrieth.

§113. See thou learn to forsake thy intimate and beloved friend for the love of God.

§114. Be not grieved when thou art forsaken by a friend, knowing that we all at length must be separated from one another.

§115. When spiritual comfort is given thee from God, receive it thankfully; but know that it is the gift of God, not thy desert.

§116. Be not puffed up, neither do thou presume vainly, but be rather the more humble for the gift, and more wary in all thine actions; for that hour will pass away, and temptation will succeed.

§117. The devil sleepeth not, neither is the flesh as yet dead; therefore cease not to prepare thyself to the battle. For on thy right hand and on thy left are enemies that never rest.

§118. Dispose thyself to patience rather than to comfort; and to the bearing of the cross rather than to joy.

§119. I willingly accept that grace whereby I may ever become more humble and careful, and more ready to renounce myself.

§120. He that desireth to keep the grace of God, let him be thankful for the grace given, and patient for the taking away thereof. Let him pray that it may return. Let him be wary and humble, lest he lose it.

§121. For where is anyone to be found that is indeed free from all affection to creatures?

§122. And if he should be very fervent in devotion, yet there is wanting one thing, which is most necessary for him.

§123. What is that? That having left all, he leave himself, and go wholly out of himself.

§124. No man richer, no man more powerful, no man more free, than he that can leave himself and all things, and set himself in the lowest place.

§125. In the cross is salvation, in the cross is life, in the cross is protection against our enemies, in the cross is heavenly sweetness, in the cross is strength of mind, in the cross is joy of spirit, in the cross is the height of virtue, in the cross is the perfection of holiness.

§126. Behold, in the cross all doth consist, and all lieth in our dying upon it; for there is no other way to life, and to true inward peace, but the way of the holy cross.

§127. Go where thou wilt, seek whatsoever thou wilt, thou shalt not find a higher way above, nor a safer way below, than the way of the holy cross.

§128. Dispose all things according to thy will and judgment; yet thou shalt ever find that thou must suffer somewhat, either willingly or against thy will, and so thou shalt ever find the cross.

§129. Thou canst not escape it, whithersoever thou runnest; for wheresoever thou goest thou carriest thyself with thee, and shalt ever find thyself.

§130. Both above and below, without and within, which way soever thou dost turn thee, everywhere thou shalt find the cross; and everywhere thou must have patience if thou wilt enjoy an everlasting crown.

§131. If thou bear the cross willingly, it will bear thee.

§132. Indeed it is not of man to bear and love the cross, to keep the body under, to fly honours, to suffer reproaches gladly, to despise himself, and to rejoice in being despised, to bear all adversities and losses, and to desire no prosperity in this world.

§133. Drink of the cup of the Lord gladly, if thou wilt be his friend.

§134. When thou shalt come to this, that tribulation shall be sweet unto thee for Christ, then think it well with thee, for thou hast found a paradise upon earth.

BOOK III

Of the Inward Speech of Christ
Unto a Faithful Soul

Christ:

§135. I am thy peace, thy life, and thy salvation.

§136. Keep thyself with me, and thou shalt find peace.

Christian:

§137. Speak, Lord, for thy servant heareth.

§138. I am thy servant, grant me understanding, that I may know thy testimonies.

§139. Incline my heart to the words of thy mouth. Let thy speech distil as the dew.

§140. [The children of Israel said unto Moses, Speak thou unto us, and we will hear thee; let not the Lord speak unto us, lest we die.]

Not so, Lord, not so, I beseech thee; but rather with the prophet Samuel I humbly and earnestly entreat, Speak, Lord, for thy servant heareth.

§141. Let not Moses speak unto me, nor any of the prophets; but do thou rather speak, O Lord God, the inspirer and enlightener of all the prophets; for thou alone without them canst perfectly instruct me; but they without thee can profit nothing.

§142. Let not therefore Moses speak unto me, but thou, my Lord God, the everlasting truth, lest I die, and prove unfruitful, if I be warned outwardly only, and not inflamed within.

§143. Speak unto me to the comfort of my soul, and to the amendment of my whole life, and to thy praise and glory, and everlasting honour.

Christ:

§144. What thou understandest not when thou readest, thou shalt know in the day of visitation.

Christian:

§145. O Lord my God, thou art to me whatsoever is good. Who am I, that I dare speak unto thee? I am thy poorest servant and a most vile worm, much more poor and contemptible than I can express.

§146. Yet remember, O Lord, that I am nothing, have nothing, and can do nothing.

§147. Remember thy mercies, and fill my heart with thy grace, thou who willest not that thy works shall be empty.

§148. Lord, teach me to fulfil thy will, teach me to live worthily and humbly in thy sight; for thou art my wisdom, thou dost truly know me, and dost know me before the world was made, and before I was born in the world.

§149. I praise thee, O heavenly Father, Father of my Lord Jesus Christ, for that thou hast vouchsafed to remember me, a poor creature.

§150. O Lord God, the holy lover of my soul, when thou shalt come into my heart, all that is within me will rejoice.

§151. Deliver me from evil passions, and heal my heart of all inordinate affections, that being healed within, I may be made fit to love, strong to suffer, and constant to persevere.

Christ:

§152. [Love is a great thing, which alone maketh every burden light, and beareth all the vicissitudes of life.]

For it carrieth a burden without a burden, and maketh everything that is bitter, sweet and savoury.

§153. Nothing is sweeter than love, nothing stronger, nothing higher, nothing more large, nothing more pleasant, nothing fuller nor better in heaven or in earth.

§154. [He that loveth, flieth, runneth, and rejoiceth; he is free and not bound.]

He giveth all for all, and hath all in all; for he resteth in the supreme God, from whom all good proceedeth.

§155. Love feeleth no burden, weigheth no pains, desireth above its strength; complaineth not of impossibility, for it thinketh all things possible.

§156. It is therefore able to undertake all things, and performeth and bringeth many things to pass; whereas he that doth not love fainteth and sinketh under them.

§157. Love watcheth, and sleeping, sleepeth not.

§158. Being tired, is not weary; straitened, is not pressed; frightened, is not disturbed; but like a lively flame it bursteth out aloft, and securely passeth through all.

Christian:

§159. Enlarge me in love, that with the inward mouth of my heart I may taste how sweet it is to love, and to be melted and swim in thy love.

§160. Let me love thee more than myself, and not myself but for thee, and all in thee that truly love thee, as the law of love commandeth, which shineth out from thee.

Christ:

§161. Love is swift, sincere, pious, pleasant, and delightful; strong, patient, faithful, prudent, long-suffering, manly, and never seeking itself.

§162. Love is circumspect, humble, and upright; not soft, nor light, nor attending unto vain things; sober, chaste, constant, quiet, and guarded in all the senses.

§163. He that is not ready to suffer all things, and to stand to the will of his beloved, is not worthy to be called a lover.

Christian:

§164. Blessed be thou, my God. For although I be unworthy of any benefits, yet thy bounty and thy infinite goodness never cease to do good even to the ungrateful, and them that are far from thee.

§165. Turn us unto thee, O Lord, that we may be thankful, humble, and holy; for thou art our power, and our strength, and our salvation.

Christ:

§166. Out of me, as out of a living fountain, the little and the great, the poor and the rich, draw the water of life; and they that willingly and freely serve me shall receive grace for grace.

Christian:

§167. O how great is the abundance of thy goodness, O Lord, which thou hast laid up for those that fear thee!

§168. But what art thou to them that love thee? What to them that serve thee with their whole heart?

§169. Truly unspeakable is the sweetness of contemplating thee, which thou bestowest on them that love thee.

§170. It ought not to seem much unto me to serve thee; but this rather seemeth much and marvellous unto me, that thou vouchsafest to receive into thy service one so poor and unworthy, and to join him with thy beloved servants.

§171. Behold, all is thine which I have, and whereby I serve thee.

§172. And yet, contrariwise, thou rather servest me than I thee.

§173. Behold, heaven and earth, which thou hast created for the service of man, are ready at hand, and all daily perform whatsoever thou dost command.

§174. And this is little. Thou hast also appointed the angels to the service of man.

§175. But that which excelleth all this is that thou thyself hast vouchsafed to serve man, and hast promised to give thyself unto him.

§176. Verily thou art my Lord, and I thy poor servant, that am bound to serve thee with all my might; neither ought I ever to be weary of praising thee.

§177. This I wish to do, this I desire; and whatsoever is wanting unto me, vouchsafe, I beseech thee, to supply.

Christ:

§178. Thou dust, learn to obey.

§179. Thou earth and clay, learn to humble thyself, to bow down beneath the feet of all men.

§180. Show thyself so lowly, such a little child, that everyone may go over thee, and tread thee as dirt under their feet.

§181. Vain man, what hast thou to complain of?

§182. Vile sinner, what canst thou answer to them who reproach thee, who hast so often offended God, and so many times deserved hell?

Christian:

§183. Use temporal things, desire eternal.

§184. Let this be my comfort, to be willing to want all human comfort.

§185. For he standeth very totteringly that casteth not his whole care upon thee.

§186. If thou vouchsafest to comfort me, be thou blessed; and if thou wilt afflict me, be thou equally blessed.

§187. Keep me from all sin, and I will neither fear death nor hell.

Christ:

§188. He is not truly patient that will not suffer but as much as he thinketh good, and by whom he listeth.

§189. But the truly patient man mindeth not by whom he is exercised, whether by his superior, or his equal, or by his inferior; whether by a good and holy man, or by a perverse and unworthy person.

§190. But indifferently from all creatures, how much soever, or how often soever, any adversity befalleth him, he taketh all thankfully from the hands of God, and esteemeth it great gain;

§191. Seeing nothing, how little soever, so it be suffered for God, shall pass without its reward from God.

Christian:

§192. Grant me, O most sweet and loving Jesus, to rest in thee above all creatures.

§193. For thou, my Lord God, art best above all; thou alone art most high, thou alone most powerful, thou alone most full and sufficient, thou alone most sweet and overflowing with comfort, thou alone most lovely and loving, thou alone most noble and glorious above all things, in whom all things are together and most perfectly, and ever have been and shall be.

§194. When shall I fully gather up myself into thee, that by reason of my love to thee I may not feel myself, but thee alone, above all sense or measure, in a manner not known unto everyone?

§195. Come, O come! for without thee I shall have no joyful hour; for thou art my joy, and without thee my table is empty.

§196. What hath thy servant more to say before thee, but greatly to humble himself in thy sight, always mindful of his own iniquity and vileness?

§197. He is as willing to be despised and condemned, and to be of no esteem or account, as to be preferred in honour before all others, and to be greater in the world.

Christ:

§198. [Son, now will I teach thee the way of peace and true liberty.]

Endeavour to do rather the will of another than thy own.

§199. Ever choose rather to have less than more.

§200. Always seek the lowest place, and to be beneath everyone.

§201. Continually wish and pray that the will of God may be wholly fulfilled in thee.

Christian:

§202. Enlighten me, O good Jesus, with a clear-shining inward light, and drive away all darkness from the habitation of my heart.

§203. Command the winds and the tempests; say unto the sea, Be still, and to the north wind, Blow not; and there shall be a great calm.

§204. Send forth thy light and thy truth, that they may shine upon the earth; for I am as the earth, without form, and void, until thou enlighten me.

§205. Pour out thy grace from above, let thy heavenly dew distil upon my heart.

§206. Supply streams of devotion, to water the face of the earth, that it may bring forth good and excellent fruit.

§207. Join me unto thee with an inseparable band of love; for thou alone dost satisfy him that loveth thee, and without thee all things are frivolous.

Christ:

§208. In everything attend unto thyself, what thou doest, and what thou sayest; and direct thy whole intention unto this, that thou mayest please me alone, and desire to seek nothing besides me.

Christian:

§209. Give me strength to resist, patience to suffer, and constancy to persevere.

Christ:

§210. If thou seekest this or that, and wouldst be here or there, to enjoy thy own will and pleasure, thou shalt never be at quiet, nor free from care;

§211. For in everything somewhat will be wanting, and in every place there will be some that will cross thee.

Christian:

§212. [Strengthen me, O God, by the grace of thy Holy Spirit . . . :]

Not to be drawn away with the desire of anything, either mean or precious, but to look upon all things as passing away, and myself as passing away together with them.

Christ:

§213. [That which I have given I can take away; and restore it again when I please.]

When I give it, it is mine; when I withdraw it, I take not anything that is thine; for mine is every good and every perfect gift.

Christian:

§214. Lord, I stand in need of yet greater grace to attain to that state wherein no man nor any creature may be a hindrance unto me.

Christ:

§215. Keep this short and perfect saying, Forsake all, and thou shalt find all. Leave desire, and thou shalt find rest.

Christian:

§216. That anything may be pleasant, thy grace must be present, and it must be seasoned with the sweetness of thy wisdom.

§217. O thou everlasting light, surpassing all created lights, dart the beams of thy brightness from above, piercing the most inward parts of my heart.

§218. Oh when will that blessed hour come when I shall be filled with thy presence, and thou be unto me all in all!

Christ:

§219. Always and every hour, as well in little things as in great, I expect nothing, but require that thou be naked and void of all things.

§220. Some also at first offer all, but afterwards, being assaulted with temptation, return again to that which they had left, and therefore they go not forward in virtue.

§221. Give all for all; seek nothing, require back nothing, abide purely and with a firm confidence in me, and then thou shalt enjoy me.

§222. Thou shalt be free in heart, and darkness shall not have any power over thee.

§223. Let this be thy prayer, let this be thy desire, that being stripped of all selfishness, thou mayst follow naked the naked Jesus, and dying to thyself, mayst live eternally with me.

§224. Look on transitory things with the left eye, and with the right behold the things of heaven.

Christian:

§225. Oh that I cleaved not too much to future events, but offered myself with all readiness of mind to thy good pleasure!

Christ:

§226. Son, if thou placest thy peace in anyone, because he thinketh like thee and liveth with thee, thou shalt be unstable and entangled.

§227. The love of thy friend ought to be grounded in me; and for me he is to be beloved, whosoever he be who is dear to thee in this life.

§228. I am he that teacheth man knowledge, and giveth unto babes a more clear understanding than can be taught by man.

§229. The time will come when the Master of masters shall appear, Christ the Lord of angels, to hear the lessons of all, that is, to examine the consciences of everyone.

§230. I am he that teach without the noise of words, without the confusion of opinions.

Christian:

§231. O Lord God, thou just Judge, strong and patient, thou who knowest the frailty and wickedness of man, be thou my strength, and my whole trust, for my own conscience sufficeth me not.

§232. Succour me, O thou the everlasting truth, that no vanity may move me.

§233. Come, heavenly sweetness, and let all impurity fly from thee.

§234. O righteous Father, and ever to be praised, the hour is come that thy servant is to be tried!

§235. It is profitable to me that shame hath covered my face, that I may the rather seek to thee for comfort than to men.

§236. Suffer me a little, that I may vent my grief, before I go unto the land of darkness, a land covered with the shadow of death.

§237. Where thou art, there is heaven; and there is death and hell where thou art not.

§238. Thou art my hope, thou art my trust, thou art my comfort, and most faithful unto me in all things.

§239. For neither can many friends avail, nor strong helpers aid, nor wise counsellors give any profitable answer, nor the books of the learned comfort, nor any wealth deliver, nor any secret or pleasant place defend, if thou thyself dost not assist, help, strengthen, comfort, instruct, and keep us.

§240. And the strongest comfort of thy servants is to trust in thee above all things.

§241. Bless and sanctify my soul with thy heavenly blessing, that it may be made thy holy habitation, and the seat of thy eternal glory.

§242. And that nothing may be found in the temple of thy glory that may offend the eyes of thy majesty.

§243. Protect and keep the soul of thy servant amidst so many dangers of this corruptible life, and by thy grace accompanying me direct it by the way of peace to the country of everlasting light. *Amen.*

BOOK IV

An Exhortation unto the Holy Communion

[*The Voice of Christ:*

Come unto me, all ye that travail and are heavy laden, and I will refresh you.]

The Voice of the Disciple:

§244. But who am I, Lord, that I should presume to approach unto thee?

§245. Behold the heaven of heavens cannot contain thee, and thou sayest, Come ye all unto me.

§246. The angels and archangels revere thee, the saints and just men fear thee, and thou sayest, Come ye all unto me.

§247. Behold Noah, a just man, laboured a hundred years in the making of the ark, that he might be saved with a few; and how can I in one hour prepare myself to receive with reverence the Maker of the world?

§248. And I, the most miserable and poorest of men, how shall I bring thee into my house, that can scarce spend one half hour devoutly? Yea, would I could once spend half an hour in a due manner!

§249. In confidence of thy goodness and mercy, I come, O Lord, a sick man unto my Saviour, hungry and thirsty to the fountain of life, needy to the King of heaven, a servant unto my Lord, a creature to my Creator, disconsolate to thee, my merciful comforter.

§250. Preserve my heart and body undefiled, that with a cheerful and pure conscience I may celebrate thy mysteries, and receive them to my everlasting health; which thou hast ordained and instituted for thy honour and for a perpetual memorial.

§251. So great, new, and joyful it ought to seem unto thee, when thou comest to these holy mysteries, as if the same day Christ, first descending into the womb of the virgin, was become man; or, hanging on the cross, did suffer and die for the salvation of mankind.

§252. Behold, O Lord, I come unto thee, that I may be comforted by thy gift, and delighted in thy holy banquet, which thou, O God, hast prepared in thy goodness for the poor.

§253. Make joyful therefore this day the soul of thy servant, for I have lifted it up unto thee, O Lord Jesus.

§254. I desire to receive thee now with devotion and reverence. I long to bring thee into my house, that with Zaccheus I may be blessed by thee, and numbered among the children of Abraham.

§255. Give me thyself, and it sufficeth; for, besides thee, no comfort is available.

§256. Let heaven and earth, and all the hosts of them, be silent in thy presence: for what praise and beauty soever they have, it is received from thy bounty, and cannot equal the beauty of thy name, of whose wisdom there is no number.

§257. My Lord God, prevent thy servant with the blessings of thy sweetness, that I may approach worthily and devoutly to thy glorious sacrament.

§258. Stir up my heart unto thee, and deliver me from a heavy numbness of mind.

§259. Visit me with thy salvation, that I may taste in spirit thy sweetness, which plentifully lieth hid in this sacrament, as in a fountain.

§260. Wherefore I implore thy mercy, and crave thy special grace, that I may wholly melt and overflow with love unto thee; and hereafter never seek any comfort out of thee.

The Voice of the Beloved:

§261. [Examine diligently thy conscience.]

So often purposing much good, and yet performing little.

§262. As I willingly offered up myself unto God my Father for thy sins, my hands being stretched forth on the cross, so that nothing remained in me that was not wholly turned into a sacrifice, for the appeasing of the divine majesty;

[So oughtest thou also to offer up thyself willingly unto me every day. . . .]

§263. I am he that hath called thee; I have commanded it to be done. I will supply what is wanting in thee: Come and receive me.

The Voice of the Disciple:

§264. Be merciful unto me, good Jesu, gracious Lord, and grant me, thy poor needy creature, to feel sometimes at least, in this holy communion, somewhat of thy tender cordial affection.

The Voice of the Beloved:

§265. Thou oughtest to seek the grace of devotion fervently, to ask it earnestly, to expect it patiently and with confidence, to receive it gratefully, to keep it humbly, to work with it diligently, and to commit the time and manner of this heavenly visitation to God, until it shall please him to come unto thee.

§266. God often giveth in a moment that which he hath a long time denied.

§267. It is sometimes a little thing that hindereth and hideth grace from us.

The Voice of the Disciple:

§268. O most loving Lord, whom I desire to receive with all devotion, thou knowest my infirmity, and the necessity which I endure, with how many evils I am oppressed, how often I am grieved, tempted, troubled, and defiled.

[I come unto thee for remedy, I crave of thee comfort and succour. . . . For thou only art my meat and my drink, my love and my joy, my sweetness and all my good.]

Selections from

Pierre Poiret

INTRODUCTION TO

Instructions for Children

John Wesley did not admire the French language, yet he looked to French piety for much spiritual inspiration. He was especially indebted to the works of Pierre Poiret (1646~1719). In 1741 he read Poiret's *Les Principes Solides de la Religion et de la Vie Chrétienne, appliqués a l'Éducation des enfans, et applicables a toutes sortes des personnes*. In these "Solid Principles of Religion and the Christian Life," Wesley found material that could indeed be applied both to children and adults, and he abridged the work to about half its original size, translating selected passages as he went along. Eventually he prepared this for publication. This may well have been the exercise to which he referred in his *Journal* for July 4, 1743: "Monday, and the following days, I had time to finish the *Instructions for Children.*" Actually, he prefixed to this a catechism for which he was partially indebted to another Frenchman, Abbé Claude Fleury (1640~1723).

Instructions for Children was in fact not published until 1745, but it was one of Wesley's most popular works, passing through ten separate editions during his lifetime, and as many afterwards. Over the course of almost thirty years Wesley linked with this work two other translated selections from French devotional writers. These he appears to have published both separately and in a composite volume, and they were reprinted in his collected *Works*. Emphasized selections from them are presented here in the order of his translation and publication of them.

The story of Wesley's gradual assembly of these three French devotional writings into one translated volume is complex, and some of the important pieces in the puzzle are still missing. We may only hint at it here. Having launched *Instructions for Children* in 1745, in 1760 Wesley inserted in volume 4 of his *Sermons* his selections from Saint-Cyran's *Christian Instructions*, and in 1761 he seems to have combined these two items into one volume, described by his printer, William Strahan of London, as "French Tracts." Two thousand copies were prepared, none of which have survived. Both items were, however, reprinted for Wesley by William Pine of

Bristol~perhaps jointly, certainly singly~and Duke University owns a volume containing a 1766 reprint of *Christian Instructions* bound up with a 1767 copy of *Instructions for Children*, both printed by Pine. In 1768 Wesley prepared a third French translation, from Jacques Joseph Duguet, entitled *Instructions for Members of Religious Societies*, of which no copy survives either as a single item or as an enlarged reissue of the French Tracts of 1761. Perkins School of Theology in Dallas, Texas, however, does own a composite volume printed by William Pine in 1772, containing all three items. From this volume they were transferred in the same order into Wesley's collected *Works*, volume 24 (1773). In this edition, the work from Poiret was entitled *Instructions for Christians*; Saint-Cyran's *Christian Instructions* was called *Christian Reflections*; and Wesley's translated selections from Duguet's *Letters on Morality and Piety* were presented under the headings of the two subjects chosen, "Instructions for Members of Religious Societies" and "Directions to Preserve Fervency of Spirit."

Wesley's asterisked extracts from *Instructions for Children* are few and brief, little more than a handful of religious aphorisms.

INSTRUCTIONS FOR CHILDREN

§1. All the men in the world cannot give us the least spark of the true knowledge of God, or of the things of God.

§2. He declares himself to those who do his will, so far as they know it already.

§3. He makes the soul in which he dwells good, wise, just, true, full of love, and of power to do well.

§4. He makes it happy. For it is his will that your soul should rejoice in him for ever. He made it for this very thing.

§5. The desire is to the soul what the mouth and the stomach are to the body.

§6. Desire was made for that which is good, that is, for God, who is the only good, and for his will, from which every good thing flows.

§7. They who teach children to love praise, train them up for the devil.

§8. We are just like the brittle vessel, which if it were not always upheld would fall at once and break in pieces.

§9. Let us ask of [God] a meek and quiet spirit, a contented, humble, thankful heart.

§10. Lord, I offer thee the desires which are wrought in me by the grace of Jesus Christ.

§11. My God, thou art good, thou art wise, thou art powerful: be thou praised for ever!

§12. A blind man, though he could reason ever so well, yet could not by this means either know or see the things of the world.

§13. In like manner, though all the men in the world should reason with all their might concerning them, yet could they not by this means know either God or the things of God.

§14. Endeavour to see God in all things, and to give a reason for everything from the perfections of God.

Selections from

Jean Duvergier

de Hauranne

(Abbé de Saint-Cyran)

INTRODUCTION TO

Christian Instructions

In 1760 John Wesley completed volume 4 of his *Sermons on Several Occasions*. There were, however, insufficient sermons at the time to make a volume comparable in size to the earlier volumes. He therefore appended other items, the last of which was entitled "Christian Instructions, extracted from a late French Author." Thus he announced the first stage of the complex publishing process by which he introduced to devout English Christians a work which he later described as "next to the Holy Scriptures" in devotional importance (*Farther Thoughts upon Christian Perfection*, introduction to part 2, later incorporated in his *Plain Account of Christian Perfection* [1766]).

The author of this work was one of the founders of Jansenism, Jean Duvergier de Hauranne (1581~1643), better known by his ecclesiastical title of Abbé de Saint-Cyran. Hauranne studied theology at the Jesuit College in Louvain, where he became a great friend of Cornelius Otto Jansen (1585~1638). He was ordained in 1618 and became Abbé of Saint-Cyran in 1620, though he lived in Paris. He earned a high reputation as a spiritual director. Many of his disciples threw in their lot with the school of thought that attacked the Roman Catholic Counter-Reformation, maintaining that a special grace from God was needed to obey his commands and that this grace was irresistible. This was based largely upon Jansen's study of Augustine, though Jansen's major work, *Augustinus*, was not published until 1640, after his death. Because of theological views and his opposition to Cardinal Richelieu, Saint-Cyran was imprisoned in 1638, but was regarded by the general public as a martyr, so that his spiritual direction was eagerly sought. He was released shortly after Richelieu's death. During his incarceration he wrote his *Lettres Chrétiennes et Spirituelles*, and the *New Catholic Encyclopaedia* notes that this work "influenced both Pascal's theology, and, through John Wesley's translation (1760), Methodist piety."

Wesley derived neither title nor text, however, from Saint-Cyran's own work, but from the editorial work of Monsieur Robert Arnauld d'Andilly (1588~1674), who in 1672 published

Instructions Chrétiennes selected from an edition of Saint-Cyran's *Lettres Chrétiennes* in two volumes. Neither the *Instructions* nor the *Lettres* were available in English; but once introduced to Saint-Cyran, Wesley selected, translated, revised, slightly rearranged, and numbered 336 spiritual "instructions," which comprised less than one-quarter of the original. It was this translation that appeared in the *Sermons* in 1760. In 1763 Wesley selected and further rearranged sixty-four of these reflections as part 2 of his *Farther Thoughts upon Christian Perfection*, whence all but the first reflection was incorporated in the *Plain Account of Christian Perfection*, thus reaching a far wider public.

Much of the work was devoted to seeking Christian perfection by means of acknowledging the nothingness of unaided man, and opening oneself to the grace of a loving God by living according to his commands, remembering always that the pure motive was more important to God than the flawed attempt: "All that a Christian does, even his eating and sleeping, is prayer, when it is done with simplicity, according to the order of God, without either adding to or diminishing from it by his own choice" (sect. 41). Constantly the spiritual thought and challenge is illuminated by natural images: "God considers our outward good works only according to the good dispositions of our hearts. And as this is sometimes like the trees in winter, full of warmth within, though producing nothing without, he loves this barrenness, caused only by outward hindrances, more than men do flowers and fruits" (sect. 43). Or this on inner peace: "The bottom of our soul may be in repose even while we are in many outward troubles; just as the bottom of the sea is calm, while the surface is strongly agitated" (sect. 69).

The closing sections are devoted to the need for, and to the personal needs of, truly spiritual ministers and preachers, whether in Roman Catholic monasteries or in Methodist societies. This at first takes one by surprise. M. Arnauld deliberately divided those 1,163 sections that he had distilled from the two volumes of Saint-Cyran's letters into two distinct parts, the first suitable for Christians in general, the second applying especially to *personnes ecclésiastiques*, though in each part he followed the ordering of the letters in the two volumes. His first part contains sections 1~1,023, his second, sections 1,024~1,163. He also furnishes an index bringing together the miscellaneous themes scattered throughout both parts. Of Wesley's 336 selections, 323 are from part 1 and 13 from part 2. Arnauld's section 1,112 (Wesley's original 323~i.e., 97 below), gives Saint-Cyran's warning that a priest offering up the sacrifice should not treat this as a commonplace duty. Wesley's methods of adapting and paraphrasing this to suit his own preachers' spiritual needs results in this final text: "A preacher should earnestly beg of God that his being accustomed to sacred offices may no ways abate the solemn awe which he at first experienced in them. There is the utmost need that he should have as much of this to the end (if not more) as at the beginning."[1]

Thus Wesley finds no problem in applying the following section: "The disposition which God indispensably requires of all that would minister his word excludes every other design but that which springs from his grace and the motion of his Spirit" (sect. 98). Wesley undoubtedly resonated to Saint-Cyran's diagnosis of the spiritual ills of his own age, so similar to those of eighteenth-century England: "Christ has always reserved in his church some ministers who bear in their souls the character of his divinity, so as to do nothing which is not suitable to his greatness, and far distant from the corruption which not only overflows the world, but even the church, the generality of his ministers" (sect. 99). He is even prepared to emphasize a passage that clearly derived from the separated religious communities of Saint-Cyran's day and denomination: "Faith has a peculiar force in an house where several souls consecrated to God are joined together" (sect. 100).[2] There was indeed good reason why Wesley felt able to employ the piety of this devout French Roman Catholic to challenge the Methodist societies of his own day, even though the latter constituted a strongly Protestant

---

[1] The original reads (we modernize the antique French): "*Un Prêtre doit extrêmement demander a Dieu que l'accoutumance de sacrifier ne le prive pas de la nouveauté de la grace dont il a toujours besoin pour sacrifier dignement.*"

[2] The French of the original reads: "*La foi qui selon S. Pierre résiste au diable a une force particulière dans ces maisons saintes ou plusieurs âmes consacrées a Dieu sont rassemblées.*"

religious community clearly living in the world rather than being separated from it. Both Saint-Cyran and Wesley were speaking without prejudice to universal spiritual problems and needs.

Almost immediately after the appearance of *Christian Instructions* in volume 4 of the *Sermons*, however, Wesley arranged for the publication of a volume incorporating that translation as its major component and title piece. This is known only from the ledgers of his printer, William Strahan of London. In December 1761 Strahan charged Wesley £6.5.0 for "French Tracts, 2½ sheets, No. 2000, large 12mo, at £2.10.0 [per sheet]." These details probably indicate a work of 60 pages, although when *Christian Instructions* was reprinted in 1766 by William Pine of Bristol it occupied 101 pages in a tiny 32mo format, which was also used for the companion publication printed by Pine in 1767, *Instructions for Children*, in 80 pages. There may well have been other editions, supporting the view expressed by Professor Orcibal: " *Christian Instructions* forms one of the chief sources of Methodist piety." (Jean Orcibal, "Les spirituels francais et espagnols chez John Wesley et ses contemporains," pp. 50~109, *Revue de L'Historie des Religions*, 1951, No. 1. See especially p. 67; cf. p. 80.)

CHRISTIAN INSTRUCTIONS

§1. The first motions of turning to God are usually like a spark of fire dropped on ice, with the wind blowing on all sides; which must therefore be quickly extinguished, unless God is pleased to keep it alive.

§2. The grace we receive soon vanishes away if it be not nourished and increased by holy exercises, which are the very first fruits, or rather the first blossoms, of conversion.

§3. The best helps to mortification are the ill usage, the affronts, and the losses which befall us. We should receive them with all humility, as preferable to all others, were it only on this account, that our will has no part therein, as it has in those which we choose for ourselves.

§4. The souls of men are things so great and precious that having need, according to the divine wisdom, of an invisible guardian, and a visible guide, they can neither have an angel to guard nor a man to guide them, but those whom God himself gives, by a peculiar appointment.

§5. The language of love and grace is upon earth the beginning of the language of heaven.

§6. Those who feel that they are always upon the verge of death, and who have eternity in their heart, will not find anything very alluring or agreeable in the world. And he to whom God is all looks on everything upon earth as nothing.

§7. True virtue consists in a thorough conformity to the whole will of God: who wills and does all (excepting sin) which comes to pass in the world. And in order to be truly holy, we have only to embrace all events, good and bad, as his will.

§8. In the greatest afflictions which can befall the just, either from heaven or earth, they remain immovable in virtue, and perfectly submissive to God, by an inward loving regard to him, uniting all the powers of their soul.

§9. Such is the condescension of God that he requires us to love him even more than we fear him. Many fear without loving him; but no one loves without fearing him, and being ready to die rather than offend him. Among persons of every age, and every profession, there are but few of this disposition; but what of piety appears in them resembles the blossoms which we see in spring, that adorn the trees for awhile, but soon disappear, and leave no fruit behind them.

§10. Whether we think or speak to God, whether we act or suffer for him, all is prayer when we have no other object than his love and the desire of pleasing him.

§11. That silence of spirit which cuts off all those thoughts and words that might spring from the affliction we feel on the loss of them who are most near and dear to us, is the best submission we can pay to that empire over the living and the dead which God has reserved to himself. And the best devotion we can practise on these occasions is, as far as possible to efface from our minds those images which disquiet and afflict us, that God alone may fill our heart, and remain forever the object and the master of our passions and of our thoughts.

§12. We ought to consider, at the death of those whom we love the most, and even of them from whom we receive life, that all the names of tenderness and respect which proceed from flesh and blood are lost at the moment of their separation from us, to return to God as their principal; to the end that the stream running no more, we may have recourse to the fountain; that ceasing to see them, we may seek to him, of whom they were only the image; and that so we may now have no other Father than him which is in heaven, of whom we are incessantly to ask the bread of life, and eternal inheritance.

§13. We ought to honour those holy ones which God honours, and to expect more assistance from them than from others at the time when he manifests their holiness; because they are then as it were new fountains, which God causes to appear in his church, and who will soon (as other saints have done) retire into God their source, after they shall have watered a few more of his children.

§14. It is scarce conceivable how strait the way is wherein God leads them that serve him, and how dependent upon him we must be, unless we will be wanting in our faithfulness to him.

§15. As a very little dust will disorder a clock, and the least sand will obscure our sight, so the least grain of sin which is upon the heart will hinder its right motion toward God.

§16. It is scarce credible of how great consequence before God the smallest things are, and what great inconveniences sometimes follow those which appear to be light faults.

§17. We ought to be in the church as the saints are in heaven; and in the house as the holiest men are in the church: doing our work in the house as they pray in the church, worshipping God from the ground of the heart.

§18. There is no love of God without patience, and no patience without lowliness and sweetness of spirit. It is by this alone that we are able to pass the days of winter as those of summer, that is, the afflictions we meet with from time to time, as well as the joys and consolations.

§19. The evils of the body cure themselves in time, but not those of the spirit; because they partake of its nature, which is immortal, and for this cure they can rely on none but God; who is the only physician of souls, as it is he alone who creates them.

§20. Agree with the poor quickly, while thou art in the way with them. Make them friends by the mammon of unrighteousness. For they will be as princes in paradise, where they will receive the rich into the everlasting habitation.

§21. God is the first object of our love; its next office is to bear the defects of others. For as he is invisible to us, it is his will that we see and love him in our neighbour. And we should begin the practice of this love amidst our own household.

§22. One observes that whereas there is but one devil who persecutes the innocent, there are seven that persecute the penitent.

§23. Humility alone unites patience with love, without which it is impossible to draw profit from suffering, or indeed to avoid being discontented at being afflicted; especially when we think that we have given no occasion for the evil which men make us suffer. If we then fall into impatience, it is for want of humility, whatever love we may appear to have.

§24. The readiest way to escape from our sufferings is to be willing they should endure as long as God pleases.

§25. As painters choose and prepare the ground which they design for their choicest works, so God prepares the ground of those souls by whom he intends to do great things. Thus he prepared St. Paul, even from his mother's womb.

§26. Nothing shows the real state of our soul like persecution and affliction. And if we suffer them with that humility and firmness which only the grace of God can work in us, we attain a larger measure of conformity to Christ, by a due improvement of one of these occasions, than we could have done by imitating his mercy, or in abundance of good works.

§27. We scarce conceive how easy it is to rob God of his due in our friendship with the most virtuous persons, until they are torn from us by death. But if this loss produce lasting sorrow, it is a clear proof that we had two treasures, between which we had divided our heart.

§28. If we do not testify to God, by a continual care for our salvation, that we esteem his grace above all things, the least consent to an evil thing makes it retire by little and little into the bosom of Christ, from whence it came. Yet he is so gracious, that after we are truly humbled, he gives us new grace.

§29. God, in order to cure some souls of those sins which are the greatest of all in his sight, suffers them to fall into others, which are greater in the sight of men.

§30. To preserve the life of the soul, prayer ought to be joined with the other ordinances, as it is the channel which reaches to heaven, and brings down into the soul that breath of God without which it cannot live.

§31. Charity cannot be practised right unless first we exercise it from the moment God gives the occasion; and secondly, retire the instant after, and offer it to God by humble thanksgiving. And this for three reasons: the first, to render to him what we have received from him; the second, to avoid the dangerous temptation which springs from the very goodness of these works; and the third, to unite ourselves to God, in whom the soul expands itself in prayer with all the graces we have received, and the good works which we have done, to draw from him new strength against the bad effects which these very works may produce in us, if we do not make use of the antidotes which God has ordained against these poisons. The true means to be filled anew with the riches of grace is thus to strip ourselves of it; and without this it is extremely difficult not to grow faint in the practice of good works.

§32. We ought to know that we have no part in the good which we do; and that accordingly, as God hides himself in doing it by us, we ought also, as far as is possible, to hide it from ourselves, and in a manner to annihilate ourselves before him, saying: "Lord, we are nothing before thee, but thou art all to us. We continue to be as nothing after thou hast by thy double mercy drawn us out of nothing and out of sin; the proof whereof we incessantly bear in ourselves, in our continual weakness and helplessness. We see ourselves in the midst of an ocean: for thou art the true and boundless ocean of nature and of grace, which neither ebbs nor flows, but is permanent and immovable. Thou spreadest abroad as it pleaseth thee the celestial waters in all ages, and drawest them back and sendest them again into the souls thou lovest, by fluxes and refluxes, ineffable and divine. Thy Spirit is the only wind that blows, and that reigns over the infinite ocean. And as we see the waters on earth which cease to run, though but for a little while, are immediately corrupted, we have reason to fear lest the same thing befall our souls, if instead of causing these heavenly waters to return to thee their source, we retain, and stop them in their motion, though it were but for a moment. For whereas the rivers of earth corrupt themselves when they stop, but without corrupting the channel through which they flow, the rivers of thy grace, though stopped, are never themselves corrupted, but the souls, the channel through which they pass. We find therefore, O God, it is more difficult to restore to thee, by an humble thankfulness, the graces we have received from thee, than to attract them into our souls by prayer; and that accordingly these refluxes toward the fountain are greater favours than the effluxes therefrom. Wherefore the only grace which we implore from thee, and which comprehends all others, is that thy grace may never descend to us but to reascend toward thee; and that it may never reascend but to descend into us again; so that we may be eternally watered by thee, and thou be eternally glorified."

§33. Good works do not receive their last perfection till they as it were lose themselves in God. This is a kind of death to them, resembling that of our bodies, which will not attain their highest life, their immortality, till they lose themselves in the glory of our souls, or rather of God, wherewith they will be filled. And it is only what they had of earthly and mortal which good works lose by spiritual death.

§34. Fire is the symbol of love; and the love of God is the principle and end of our good works. But as truth surpasses figure, the fire of divine love has this advantage over material fire, that it can reascend to its source, and rise thither with all the good works which it produces. And by this means it prevents their being corrupted by pride, vanity, or any evil mixture. But this cannot be done otherwise than by making these good works in a spiritual manner die in God, by deep gratitude, which plunges the soul in him as in an abyss, with all that it is, and all the grace and works for which it is indebted to him; a gratitude whereby the soul seems to empty itself of them, that they may return to their source, as rivers seem willing to empty themselves when they pour themselves with all their waters into the sea.

§35. When we have received any favour from God, we ought to retire (if not into our closet, into our heart) and say: "I come, Lord, to restore to thee what thou hast given, and I freely relinquish it, to enter again into my own nothingness. For what is the most perfect creature in heaven or earth in thy presence, but a void capable of being filled with thee and by thee, as the air which is void and dark is capable of being filled with the light of the sun? Grant therefore, O God, that I may never appropriate thy grace to myself, any more than the air appropriates to itself the light of the sun; who withdraws it every day to restore it the next, there being nothing in the air that either appropriates its light or resists it. Oh, give me the same facility of receiving and restoring thy grace and good works. I say thine, for I acknowledge the root from which they spring is in thee, and not in me."

§36. As all that we can properly call our own is the evil which is natural to us, they who are truly touched by the Spirit of God have no right to complain of any reproach, whether they are guilty of the thing or not. It suffices that they have in them the principle of all the faults which are or can be laid to their charge.

§37. We should chiefly exercise our love toward those who most check either our way of thinking, or our temper, or our knowledge, or the desire we have that others should be as virtuous as we would wish to be ourselves.

§38. As God once subsisted without any creature in his own infinite fullness, so love will one day subsist in itself, without any outward works: which are now only the streams whereof love is the source, the shoots of which this is the root, the rays whereof love is the sun, the spark of which this is the fire, always acting, always consuming, and yet preserving the soul wherein it dwells.

§39. The desire of exercising charity obliges us to purify ourselves by all sorts of holy exercises, that we may be filled with the gifts of God, and capable of imparting them to others without losing anything of our own fullness. By thus exercising our charity we increase it. This alone, when it fills the heart, has the advantage of giving always, and by giving enriching itself.

§40. All is clear to us in proportion as we walk in the bright path of faith, obedience, prayer, love, and Christian fidelity.

§41. All that a Christian does, even his eating and sleeping, is prayer, when it is done with simplicity, according to the order of God, without either adding to or diminishing from it by his own choice.

§42. The three greatest punishments which God can inflict on sinners in this world are: (1) to let loose their own desires upon them; (2) to let them succeed in all they wish for; and (3) to suffer them to continue many years in the quiet enjoyment thereof.

§43. God considers our outward good works only according to the good dispositions of our hearts. And as this is sometimes like the trees in winter, full of warmth within, though producing nothing without, he loves this barrenness, caused only by outward hindrances, more than men do flowers and fruits.

§44. Love shows courtesy to young and old, good and bad, wise and unwise: indeed to all the world. But it uses no flattery either to others or ourselves.

§45. Love fasts when it can, and as much as it can. It leads to all the ordinances of God, and employs itself in all the outward works whereof it is capable.

It flies, as it were, like Elijah, over the plain, to find God upon his holy mountain.

§46. We ought to suffer with patience whatever befalls us, to bear the defects of others, and our own, to own them to God in secret prayer, or with groans which cannot be uttered: but never to speak a sharp or peevish word, nor to murmur or repine.

§47. The sea is an excellent figure of the fullness of God, and that of the blessed spirits. For as the rivers all return into the sea, so the bodies, the souls, and the good works of the righteous return into God, to live there in his eternal repose.

§48. What the Scripture terms "the finger of God" is no other than the Holy Spirit, who engraves in our hearts what pleaseth him.

§49. It is full as glorious to die for charity as for truth; nor will it have a less recompense from God.

§50. Death entered by the ear into the soul of our first mother: by the eye chiefly it enters the souls of her children. But whereas Eve, after having hearkened to the serpent, took the forbidden fruit, her children generally, after having seen it, hearken to the counsels of the devil. And indeed, if the few words of that unhappy spirit ruined Eve, even in a state of innocence, what can we expect if in our state of sin and impotence we pass our life in perpetual converse with the world, and in the continual sight of creatures under which the devil conceals himself far better than under the form of a serpent?

§51. To conceive still better the danger we are in while we remain in the corruption of the world, consider on the one hand Eve, with her strength and innocence in the paradise of God; on the other men, weak and sinful; the creatures, all infectious, all instruments of sin, and that are as a veil with which the devil covers himself, to tempt us the more effectually; and lastly, the world, which is the place of banishment with regard to our bodies, a prison with regard to our souls, and an hell with regard to those evil spirits who remain there, continually mingled with men, till the judgment of the great day.

§52. The great will, after their death, look upon the pomp and pleasures wherein they had lived just as those who awake from a deep sleep do on the riches, honours, and pleasures which they saw in their dream.

§53. As on many occasions some of the senses correct the others, and reason corrects them all; so faith, which is in Christians a superior reason, ought to correct the judgment which purely human reason forms of the goods and evils of this world.

§54. All that is good here below flows from above. And if but one drop could fall into our heart of the happiness of heaven, pure as it is in its source, earth would become a paradise. Nor would there be then need to put off the body; because the least part of those heavenly goods, received in its fullness, would render us blessed and immortal, even in this world.

§55. Although all the grace of God depends on his mere bounty, yet is he pleased generally to attach them to the prayers, and good instructions, the good examples, and the holiness, of those among whom we are brought up. And if we knew the secret of the grace of Christ, and the strong though invisible attractions whereby he draws some souls through their intercourse with others, we should beware to whom we entrusted the education of our children.

§56. To prepare the mind for prayer it ought to be at liberty, in tranquillity, in humility, in confidence, in simplicity, and in an entire dependence on God: not troubled, not divided, not wavering, neither preventing the will of God by any secret passion.

§57. Prayer continues in the desire of the heart, though the understanding be employed on outward things.

§58. God's command to pray without ceasing is founded on the necessity we have of his grace, to preserve the life of God in our soul, which can no more subsist one moment without it than the body can subsist without continual supplies of air.

§59. As the most dangerous winds may enter at little openings, so the devil never enters more dangerously into the souls of good men than by little amusements, and little unobserved incidents, which, seeming to be nothing, yet insensibly open the heart to great temptations.

§60. The chief desire of Christian parents should be for the salvation of their children. Without this, all they do for them serves only to draw the curse of God upon themselves; since they are as guardian angels that ought to conduct to heaven those to whom they have given life. 'Tis a great mistake to suppose they can please God by any other good works while they neglect this.

§61. The perfection we are incessantly to press after is no other than perfect love; and love cannot increase in the soul but by a disengagement from sensible and pleasing objects. Otherwise our love is false, our courtesy deceitful, and our condescension to others only a snare to ourselves; because instead of flowing from the love of God, they flow from self-love, and the love of the world.

§62. The readiest way which God takes to draw a man to himself is to afflict him in that which he loves the most, and with good reason; and to cause this affliction to arise from some good action done from a single eye; because nothing can more clearly show him the emptiness of what is most lovely and desirable in the world.

§63. God does nothing but in answer to prayer; and even those who have been converted to God without praying for it themselves (which is exceeding rare), were not without the prayers of others.

§64. To prayer should be added continual employment; for grace fills a vacuum as well as nature, and the devil fills whatever God does not fill.

§65. One of the greatest faults which parents can commit, and which is the source of numberless disorders in families and in commonwealths, is that instead of bringing up their children as those that are now the children of God, by the second birth which they received in baptism, they think only of giving them such an education as is suitable to their first birth. They take great care of them as they are children of Adam, but none at all as they are children of God. Thus they are murderers of their own children, stifling the life of God which was begun in their souls.

§66. Uniformity of life and symmetry of action is essential to Christian holiness. It is like a circle, which is considered as the first of figures because of the equality of all its parts.

§67. It is highly dangerous to grow in the knowledge of the things of God, and not in the love of God.

§68. God does not love men that are inconstant, nor good works that are intermitted. Nothing is pleasing to him but what has a resemblance of his own immutability.

§69. The bottom of our soul may be in repose, even while we are in many outward troubles; just as the bottom of the sea is calm, while the surface is strongly agitated.

§70. God frequently conceals the part which his children have in the conversion of other souls. Yet one may boldly say that a person who long groans before him for the conversion of another, whenever the soul is converted to God, is one of the chief causes of it; especially if it is a mother who prays and groans for her child.

§71. A constant attention to the work with which God entrusts us is the greatest mark of solid piety.

§72. We are to bear with those whom we cannot amend, and to be content with offering them to God. There is no greater exercise of charity than this, nor of true resignation. And since God has borne our infirmities in his own person, we may well bear those of each other for his sake.

§73. Nothing is more to be lamented than that the wounds of the soul are invisible like herself; and that we are so far from being sensible of them as soon as we have received them, that for a long time we find pleasure in our misfortune, and fancy we are well, though we are sick unto death.

§74. As devils and the souls of men are both of the same, of a spiritual nature, and accordingly the former well understand what passes in the latter, they find it easy to transmit from one soul to another the corruption and infection they meet with there, by means of the evil conversation and friendly intercourse there is between them.

§75. The fears which the first appearance of the great truths of God raise in the minds of young converts resemble those which are occasioned at first by the apparition of good angels; but they soon pass away, and leave the soul in peace and joy in the Holy Ghost.

§76. Jesus Christ renews his own life every hour in the bodies and souls of real Christians. They are living images of him, and represent him in a more excellent manner than the writings of the gospel itself. For the dead characters of the gospel (though living in another sense) contain only the past life of Christ; whereas true Christians contain also his present life, and that in living characters: which caused the Apostle to declare, "I live not, but Christ liveth in me" [Gal. 2:20].

§77. It is not good for a babe in Christ either to converse much with the world, or to be wholly alone.

§78. Employment frequently holds the place of mortification, and produces the same effects.

§79. Our continuance in good works is the best means to retain a continual sense of the love of God.

§80. The sympathies formed by grace far surpass those formed by nature.

§81. God considers us only according to what we are in our hearts, in the secret movements of our soul, in our hidden intentions and our passions imperceptible to others. The goodness of all our works depends on the purity and simplicity of our heart, which is as it were the spirit, the invisible soul of this visible body.

§82. If we do not devote all we do to God, there is nothing in our best works but what is human or pagan; because we regard only ourselves therein, and while we do what is good in appearance, we in effect put ourselves by a secret self-complacence in the place of God.

§83. Thanksgiving is as it were the soul of prayer, with which it should begin, continue, and end.

§84. God frequently gives a soul that ardently loves him a dispensation from those laborious works which it would do, to testify its gratitude by laying obstacles in the way which makes them impossible.

§85. Nothing is more true than that "The yoke of Christ is easy, and his burden light" [cf. Matt. 11:30]. For one need only love to fulfil the whole law, even when it cannot be outwardly accomplished. And yet it is true that this dispensation from outward works, which proceeds from providential hindrances, is often a greater trial to souls full of love than the most painful of those works would have been.

§86. As the furious hate which the devil bears us is termed, the roaring of the lion, so our vehement love may be termed, crying after God.

§87. A soul returned to God ought to be attentive to everything which is said to him on the head of salvation, with a secret desire to profit thereby.

§88. If the love of God does not increase in us in the same degree as we increase in knowledge, the stronger principle will overcome the weaker, and knowledge will stifle love. This has occasioned men of the greatest learning almost to envy their happiness who know little, but love much.

§89. The body increases without decreasing, till it comes to a certain age. But there is no limited time wherein the soul may not either increase or decrease.

§90. If one cannot faithfully serve an earthly prince without exposing himself to many dangers in his court, and to death in his armies, it is far more reasonable that those who serve God in the church, which is the court of his Son, should expose themselves to all the dangers, and suffer all the evils, that occur in his service; especially as he who has established this kingdom was himself hated of men, and has foretold that the war which they who preached the gospel after him need make upon the world, would cause them likewise to be hated of all men for his name's sake.

§91. A true guide of souls ought to be as the heart, the tongue, and the hand of God, to labour by his assistance for the salvation of them that are under his care. For it is not he that prays, that speaks, that wishes, strives, suffers; but it is the Spirit of God which does all this, when the minister is united to him, and calls upon him continually.

§92. There ought nothing to come out of the mouth or the heart of a preacher of the gospel but what is not only reasonable but Christian, and animated by the Holy Spirit.

§93. Between the physicians of the soul and those of the body there is a great difference in this. The latter are more and more hardened by the sight of more patients and diseases; whereas the hearts of the former, by the sight of spiritual diseases, grow more and more tender.

§94. The only way to undertake the preaching of the gospel is to enter upon it by the inspiration of God, without having any regard to the world, or of what is either agreeable or disagreeable in it, and to forget even our own house and relations, just as Abraham did, in order to love God alone, as if he alone were our world, our relations, our all.

§95. It is the glory of all true ministers of Christ to resemble the angels of God. They nearly resemble them by having renounced the body, in order to regard the soul only; by their life all spiritual, uniform throughout, all from God, all for God, and all proceeding from the Spirit of God, as is that of the angels in heaven.

§96. He who is honoured with the ministry ought to be and to appear as far separate from common Christians as common Christians ought to be and to appear separate from heathens.

§97. A preacher should earnestly beg of God that his being accustomed to sacred offices may no ways abate the solemn awe which he at first experienced in them. There is the utmost need that he should have as much of this to the end (if not more) as at the beginning.

§98. The disposition which God indispensably requires of all that would minister his word excludes every other design but that which springs from his grace and the motion of his Spirit.

§99. Christ has always reserved in his church some ministers who bear in their souls the character of his divinity, so as to do nothing which is not suitable to his greatness, and far distant from the corruption which not only overflows the world, but even the church, the generality of his ministers.

§100. Faith has a peculiar force in an house where several souls consecrated to God are joined together.

§101. [The life of a minister ought to be uniform, to render it exemplary.] And if his example does not edify the world, neither will his writing benefit the Church.

§102. When anyone writes for God, he should seek for no other eloquence than that which God gives in the simplicity of his Spirit. He would corrupt this were he to mix it with human eloquence; and he should never forget, before, in, and after his work, to cry to God that he may have his heart continually lifted up to him who ought to be the source of all the thoughts and all the conversation of every minister.

§103. While a man is alienated from God, he makes little account of that natural inclination which such an one has to some good works, or his aversion to some sins. But from the moment that he is converted to God, he sanctifies this inclination and this aversion, and serves himself of it in order to increase it; and nevertheless, the ease with which we do those good works, and avoid those evil ones, does not at all diminish the reward or value of them. Thus what was only virtuous heathenism before becomes true Christian virtue, by the infusion of love, which is in us as it were a second soul, all divine, and which transforms into itself that which before animated the body.

§104. How clear-sighted soever a man is in other respects, he hardly sees all that love requires to be done, whether in respect of God or his neighbour, but while he feels that love in his heart.

Selections from

Jacques Joseph Duguet

INTRODUCTION TO
Letters on Morality and Piety

In his *Journal* for February 26, 1768, Wesley wrote: "I translated from the French one of the most useful tracts I ever saw, for those who desire to be 'fervent in spirit.' How little does God regard men's opinions! What a multitude of wrong opinions are embraced by all the members of the Church of Rome! Yet how highly favoured have many of them been!" Dr. Jean Orcibal has shown that the work which Wesley read~again one which had never been translated into English~was *Lettres sur divers sujets de morale et de piété* (Jean Orcibal, "Les spirituels francais . . . ," as noted above, especially pp. 67~68, 99~101). The author was Jacques Joseph Duguet (1649~1733), a prolific Jansenist writer. After a noviciate in the Oratory of Paris he was ordained priest in 1677 but resigned from his pastoral and teaching labors in 1685, refusing to sign a form declaring his repudiation of Jansenism. Henceforth he devoted himself to writing alone~controversial theology, exegetical studies, and devotional works (*Dictionnaire de Spiritualité*, Tome III, Paris: Beauchesne, 1957, pp. 1759~70).

Duguet's *Lettres* were first published in Paris in 1708, without his name, but simply a note, "par l'auteur du Traité de la Priere publique." His *Treatise on Public Prayer* had been published earlier that same year. The letters were frequently reprinted and gradually expanded in size and number of volumes. Wesley may well have been introduced to the work by Miss Freeman, an intelligent and devout woman whom he had known from her childhood, and who spoke French so fluently that on April 18, 1760, Wesley took her with him on a pastoral visit to the French prisoners of war in Dublin, when they "were surprised at hearing as good French spoke in Dublin as they could have heard in Paris." Among Wesley's own annotated volumes in Wesley's House, London, is the sixth edition (1719) of Duguet's *Lettres*, with Wesley's own inscription: "JW. Given by Miss Freeman, 1770." If this date is correct, however, the presentation volume would seem to have been a replacement for Wesley of the original edition from which he had translated and published his selections, for his extracts were dated 1768.

Wesley selected passages from the first two of the fourteen letters originally published, and on November 7, 1771, quoted also (in a letter to Nancy Bolton) passages from the third letter. The first letter dealt with the conduct of novices in a Roman Catholic community, "Instructions sur la manière de conduire les novices." This Wesley presented as "Instructions for Members of Religious Societies." He made no attempt to disguise his source, however, pointing out in a footnote: "This letter was originally designed for those of a Religious House in France." The second was entitled "Avis propres a rétablir et a conserver dans une religieuse une piété sincere et fervente," which Wesley described as "Directions to Preserve Fervency of Spirit."

The translations appeared in 1773, in volume 24 of Wesley's collected *Works*, where they are dated at the end, "London, Feb. 26, 1768." That this was not their first publication, however, is implied by his letter to Miss Mary Bosanquet on January 2, 1770: "I suppose you have the 'Instructions for Members of Religious Societies.' I know nothing equal to them in the English tongue. It would be well diligently to inculcate those Instructions on all under your roof"~i.e., in the tiny religious community which she maintained in her own home near Leeds, Yorkshire. But no copy of the presumed 1768 volume first incorporating this work with its two predecessors appears to have survived, no more than has the first "French Tracts" printed by William Strahan for Wesley in 1761. In the Perkins School of Theology, Dallas, Texas, however, one copy of the new threefold work still remains. It is entitled *Instructions for Christians*, and it uses that title both for the first part (in fact, the earlier *Instructions for Children*) and the second (*Christian Instructions*), to which are added both extracts from Duguet on pages 181~213. The following year Pine incorporated this compilation into Wesley's *Works*, and Wesley continued to recommend them to his followers, as to Elizabeth Ritchie in a letter of July 31, 1774: "The unction of the Holy One will shine in your heart and shine upon your path, especially if you frequently consider the 'Directions for preserving Fervency of Spirit' and the 'Farther Thoughts upon Christian Perfection.'"

As may be seen in the appendix of sources, Wesley utilized only selections from the third and fourth parts of Duguet's lengthy first letter and only half of the numbered sections of the shorter second letter. Sometimes he offered a paraphrase, though always the source remains indisputable. Frequently Wesley sharpens Duguet's writing by breaking up his lengthier sentences and presenting their substance in his own much crisper style. On some occasions, however, Wesley's translation of the French is heavily literal and somewhat awkward. Thus his slavish rendering of *si* as *so* four times in the opening sentence on chastity (sect. 1) fails to convey the meaning of the original French. Usually, however, Wesley successfully transmits Duguet's compressed spiritual wisdom, as may be exemplified by two passages from Letter II. The first comes from section 2: "Be always faithful to your conscience, to the first cry of charity, to that clear decision which you hear in your heart upon every duty. Do not confound with your reason this supreme rule of reason. Reverence it as the voice of God."[1] And then the whole of section 9: "When you are doing a thing, never depend on doing it better another time; but at this time give it all possible attention. When you are doing one thing, do not think on another that is to follow it. Always limit yourself to the present moment, and distrust projects which cause you to slight the present work by promising wonders in time to come."[2]

---

[1] "*Soyez toujours fidèle à vôtre conscience, à ce premier crie de la charité, à cette décision nette et précise que vous entendez dans vôtre coeur sur chaque devoir. Ne confondez pas avec vôtre raison cette règle suprême de la raison, respectez-là comme la voix de Dieu . . . .*"

[2] "*Ne vous proposez jamais, lorsque vous ferez une chose, de la faire mieux dans un autre temps, et donnez-lui dès lors toute l'attention nécessaire. Ne vous occupez point dans une action de celle qui la suivra. Bornez-vous toujours au moment présent; et défiez-vous des projets qui enlevent toujours au moment présent, en promettant des merveilles pour l'avenir.*"

LETTERS ON MORALITY AND PIETY

I

Instructions for Members of Religious Societies

§1. [Members of religious societies, who ought to be so holy, who have so many helps for becoming so, frequently fall short of it through the excessive confidence they are taught to place in external rules. They do not know that true holiness flows neither from the will nor from the efforts of man. They are not sensible that their corruption is above all remedies except only the grace of Christ; that all outward helps reach not the deep and invisible wound of the heart, and that they are desperately sick who fancy they can be cured by their own cares or labours. These do not hold by the root of all true good, which is Jesus Christ. . . . This is therefore highly needful for them to consider, that neither *the staff of the prophet* nor *his servant* is able to raise the dead (2 Kings 4:18~37), but only the prophet himself stretched upon the body~that is, Christ become man for us.

[It is of deep importance that they should understand the connection there is between their vows and the gospel.] Suppose they did not vow obedience to their Superior, they must dread their own will as the source of all vices. For in any state we are not at our own disposal, we are not to live to ourselves, or permitted to rest in ourselves, or to be our own rule and end.

We need not make a vow of poverty; but in every state the love of riches is forbidden; covetousness is idolatry; and trust in our goods is incompatible with a due trust in God. We must limit ourselves to the necessities of nature; dispense the rest with the most exact fidelity, and use even what we allow ourselves as though we used it not.

We need not bind ourselves to a single life: but the laws of chastity are so strict in every state; faults of this kind are so dangerous; the occasions of them are so frequent in the world; and it is so just to be afraid of that sin which may be committed even by a look, that it is easier to abstain from all than to stop precisely at the point where innocence ends. See what is the ground of resolving upon a single life. And we should infinitely deceive ourselves if we regarded chastity as a thing indifferent,

before we made the resolution. The dangers we are in, an holy
fear, the care of an inestimable treasure lodged in a brittle
vessel, and the desire of pleasing Christ by giving him an
undivided heart, were, or ought to have been, our only motives
for making such a resolution. It is because we do not conceive
this that we are so little guarded against the tender connections,
and so feebly resist that desire of pleasing; so often attach
ourselves to persons whom we ought not to see, but in order to
become more pure; that we nourish in our hearts a thousand
useless and frivolous desires; suffer our comfort to depend on the
most trifling things; and fall into the incomprehensible folly of
having renounced what is lawful, the love of a spouse, and of
children, to put silly, little, forbidden attachments in the place
of these innocent and even holy ties.

§2. It is then of great moment to distinguish between those
rules which seem purely arbitrary, and those which all must
impose upon themselves if they purpose to save their souls. Such
are stated hours of private prayer, reading, and meditation;
constant and serious employment; plain and modest apparel,
and a carriage still more plain and modest; a steady uniformity of
behaviour; following the counsel of some guide who is taught of
God; an habitual dread of softness and pleasure, and a love of
penitence. Nothing of this is arbitrary. Piety partly consists in
these things, partly depends upon them. If you was in no
religious society, you would be equally obliged to these, but you
would be deprived of the valuable helps of rule, of instruction,
and of example, which you now enjoy.

§3. And even those rules which appear quite arbitrary and
indifferent are usually necessary in order to the keeping of
others, as the husk preserves the corn, and as the letter preserves
the spirit. It seems indeed to men of the world that these are
little things; but pride and worldly wisdom are ill judges of what
is little or great in the eyes of God. There are abundance of
things necessary in order to discipline, precious helps for
humility and fervency of spirit, which the world despises, but
which the children of God know the value of.

§4. Above all things, we must labour to convince ourselves
thoroughly that we can never fill up the character of a life
consecrated to the service of God without an universal

renunciation of all things; that it avails nothing to shut all the other gates, if we leave one open for the devil; that we only make him rage the more unless we resist him, more valiantly in every point; that the least vice indulged brings back all the rest; that the self-love which leads us to except anything leads us afterwards to resume all; that whatever takes up a part of our heart necessarily wounds and weakens it; that the parting it, when we owe and have promised the whole, is no less than sacrilege; that the death of Ananias ought to make all those tremble who keep back a part; that the command to Lot and his wife, *not to look back*, is renewed by Christ in the gospel; that it is easy, by our desires, to turn back to the world; and that one cannot even thus return to it without rendering ourselves unworthy to enter into the promised land; that we cannot conceive the fury of the devil against those who undertake to live an angelic life in a mortal body; we cannot conceive therefore how necessary it is to redouble our vigilance against his unwearied efforts, and to be as unwearied and as diligent as him; otherwise he must prevail.

§5. Let us be thoroughly persuaded that Christianity implies a general opposition to all the false notions of the world, to its maxims and sentiments; that it knows no other pattern than Jesus Christ and him crucified; that his disgraces and griefs are all its riches, and all its consolations; that consequently nothing is more opposite thereto than pride and the love of pleasures, and that the only way for Christians to become great is to be sincerely willing to be the least of all; that is, the most unknown, the most despised, the most dependent, the least accommodated, and yet the most patient and the most satisfied; not through an idea of our own virtue, which would be the height of pride, but from a consciousness of our own unworthiness, and from a deep love of the truth, which makes us sensible of it.

§6. Accustom yourself to do nothing without design, without reflection, without a lively sentiment of piety: not to suffer any of your actions to be lost; not to lose the fruit of any of your prayers; never to appear before God in public service without summoning all your faith; to esteem nothing great but for the holy dispositions with which it is performed; never to

separate your actions or your sufferings from those of Jesus
Christ, from which they derive all their value; to count for
nothing all, either virtue or wisdom, which is not grounded on
Jesus Christ, which has more of show than of truth, which swells
self-love, not the love of God; to distrust all virtues which do
not render you more humble, more detached from yourselves,
more ready to yield to all the world. To dread in that which is
good the vain satisfaction which is almost inseparable, and
which is the poison of it. To be truly humbled by your faults; to
preserve with great care the desire of future bliss, the sense of
the mercies of God, the remembrance of your sins and miseries,
and the spirit of compunction, which is the very soul of religion.

§7. Guard early against the temptations and dangers which
might one day weaken you. Few continue as they have begun;
fewer advance in virtue. There are, even in the most holy
retreats, what are almost certain means of enfeebling the soul;
and it is a great misfortune either not to know them, or when
one does know them, not to guard against them. It is impossible
to set down here everything which may slacken the soul. A
thousand imperceptible ways, a thousand imperceptible declen-
sions, a thousand slight losses, a thousand secret snares, may
occasion this. Natural inconstancy and fickleness, lukewarmness
in prayer, union with persons that are not fervent in spirit,
attachment to anything wrong, which God punishes; the
slighting of little duties, of little faults, of the checks of an
enlightened conscience; the forgetting the reasons and motives
which induced us to choose the state wherein we are; a secret
disgust at our superior; too quick a sense of some slight or refusal;
too great liberty in examining the defects of our brethren;
listening to murmurers; any secret unfaithfulness not acknowl-
edged; anything done with a doubting conscience; any temptation on which we have not had the humility to ask advice; any
fear of raillery in doing our duty; any slight dissipation; but
above all any secret pride: for it is this sin which almost always
leads to the rest. And one cannot too much recommend to them
who would be all devoted to God an humility proportioned to
the graces they have need of in order to advance in virtue and
persevere to the end.

§8. As persons usually know only the outside of chastity, and are little informed of its inward ground and its extent, it is of importance to consider that this virtue resides chiefly in the heart; that it extinguishes all desire to have a place in the heart of another; that it is an enemy to pleasure, to all that gratifies the senses, to all superfluity, to all that satisfies curiosity or softness, to all that weakens the soul and makes it bend earthward, to all that wounds the most severe modesty, to all that disturbs the peace and tranquillity necessary for prayer, to all that is capable of creating or recalling dangerous images; in fine to all that strengthens the chains which attach the soul to the body, and the inclination which it is so hard to lay aside of seeking our repose in sensible things.

§9. In order to be agreeable in a family, we ought not to suffer in ourselves any defect which we can correct. We should be neat in our clothes, in our chamber, in all that we do either for ourselves or others. Our gait, our way of speaking, our whole behaviour, should be reformed with care. There may be much of simplicity therein, and yet much of dignity. We should not give ourselves leave to laugh, to speak, to admire anything, in a flat and disgusting manner. We should carefully avoid everything that is coarse, clownish, or indecent, and every way of expressing joy or friendship which is not quite well-bred and modest. Shun betimes little habits which give pain to others, and which age and negligence may increase. Accustom yourself to reflect upon everything which might incommode another; to avoid [it] with care, and not to slide into it either through hurry or forgetfulness. On the other side, we ought to bear with sweetness whatever incommodes us in another; to exact nothing; to excuse everything, and to be patient ourselves, and studious for the good of the family, purely from a motive of Christian love; regarding as mere worldly politeness whatever is done with a lower view, or from purely human motives.

§10. The chief dispositions of mind which are necessary in every member of a Christian family are goodness, sweetness, patience, the desire of obliging, the fear of grieving or hurting anyone, a care to preserve love in himself and others; a pain to see any breach therein; humanity toward the weak either in mind or in body; a joy in taking the burdens of others upon ourselves; a love of the religious exercises which are performed in common; and avoiding all needless singularity; an unspeakable aversion to complaints and murmurs; a sincere, respectful, and tender union, first with our superior, and afterwards with all our brethren. We cannot but bestow different degrees of love and esteem upon these, according to their different gifts and graces, but we should be very wary as to the public marks whereby we show our inward preference of some to others.

II

Directions to Preserve Fervency of Spirit

§1. If we would preserve our fervour unabated, we must particularly attend to those things which have at all times led to weariness and weakness of spirit, and to those which tend to inspire zeal and fervour, and to rekindle languid desires. We should regard the former as certain mischiefs, whatever pretences may be made to excuse them, and the latter as invaluable helps, however little or trifling they may appear to false wisdom.

§2. Frequently reflect on the insensible decays by which our piety is weakened. Dread the consequences of the least relaxations, which at the beginning appear so far removed from the point to which they lead. Be assured that all faults which are neglected are punished, the little ones by great, the inward by outward, lukewarmness by insensibility. Be always faithful to your conscience, to the first cry of charity, to that clear decision which you hear in your heart upon every duty. Do not confound with your reason this supreme rule of reason. Reverence it as the voice of God. Do not deliberate on the obedience you owe to it. Give no entrance to the enemy, by reasoning upon any command or prohibition of the Holy Spirit. By resisting the beginning of temptations, you easily conquer them, whereas after the first moment you are almost disarmed and vanquished.

§3. Make it a point of duty to do nothing out of humour, that is, without any reason but inclination. Be faithful in the use of every means, independently on relish or disrelish. When you are heavy, look for the return of grace and unction; when you have most fervour, prepare for temptation. Look on these inward vicissitudes as you do on those of bodily health. Do not neglect them; and yet beware of being discouraged thereby.

Only redouble your diligence and your care in proportion to the length and violence of your trials. And from the moment that light appears again, be so humble and so thankful that you may keep it.

§4. The esteem, confidence, and friendship of others serve only to weaken you if they lessen that compunction and contempt of yourself which is the source of true strength. Unless love or necessity require it, be not forward to talk of those things which you know the best. Esteem simplicity and purity of heart more than the finest understanding. Do not cherish the desire of either having or showing this. Never show in your conversation an air of capacity and sufficiency. Cure the prejudices of persons less enlightened than you by a modest, calm, loving behaviour, and draw no other advantage from being more knowing than that of being more humble.

§5. Be sweet, even, courteous, from a motive of faith and love, not from a desire to please. The more capable virtues of this kind are of attracting esteem and friendship, the more vigilance and jealousy over ourselves is needful that they may be pure and holy. For it is easy to seduce the heart of others, even though we are clear ourselves. And it is a great affliction to one who loves God to be the occasion of another's loving him less, or in a less noble and less perfect manner.

§6. Regard then those advantages which draw love and esteem only as snares and sources of temptation, without that extraordinary grace which is seldom given, because men are seldom humble enough to obtain it. Be abased before God for whatever distinguishes you in the sight of men, as it exposes you to pride, the most shameful of all vices in a poor, sinful wretch. Esteem only that which God esteems; praise only that which he praises. Make little account of all the shining virtues which are found even in reprobates. Regard piety and humility as the only ones which distinguish the children of God from the children of wrath.

§7. Preserve with the utmost care the spirit of piety, recollection, watchfulness, and compunction. Do nothing in haste and with dissipation. Speak nothing but what is necessary. Never speak without watching over your words and the motive which leads you to speak. Talk not even on useful subjects but with a single eye; otherwise you may lose the treasure which is in your heart by showing it from a wrong motive.

§8. Let none of your actions, not even the smallest, be lost. Do them all from views which spring from faith. Accordingly, know why you do them. Do not walk by chance, without seeing your mark or without aiming at it. Despise nothing, because every action may become of great price. Make all noble, all grand, all divine. Nothing is little when one loves much, and nothing is great when one loves but little.

§9. When you are doing a thing, never depend on doing it better another time; but at this time give it all possible attention. When you are doing one thing, do not think on another that is to follow it. Always limit yourself to the present moment, and distrust projects which cause you to slight the present work, by promising wonders in time to come.

§10. Do not wait till the evening before you examine all your actions and all your motives. Keep one part of your soul continually attentive on what the other does. Let not your whole soul be taken up with anything except prayer, which is then most pure when one least reflects upon it. Never lose serenity of mind and peace of heart; because when your soul is ruffled you no longer know what you do, whither you go, nor where your danger lies. Stop the very moment you begin to be no longer your own master. That moment fly to prayer, and continue therein till peace returns to your soul.

§11. Never be under so much apprehension as when you do any good, when you speak with wisdom and reason; because you are then on the brink of that most slippery and dangerous precipice, vanity. After having felt more fervour and enlargement of heart in any ordinance, or having suffered anything with more patience and sweetness than usual, labour to be more humble; for the devil is watching to steal away the fruit as soon as it appears: and it is just in God to suffer it so to be, if you are robbing him of his glory. Always receive commendations and marks of esteem with a secret reluctance, for fear lest God should blast these vain applauses with an hidden curse. On the contrary, esteem yourself happy in being neglected, despised, yea, reproached, how severely soever; because God generally shows himself most present and most gracious at those precious moments.

APPENDIX

The Sources of Wesley's Selections
Thomas `a Kempis, The Christian's Pattern

Shown here after the section numbers are the corresponding details of sources: (a) Wesley's complete edition of a Kempis, 1735; (b) Wesley's *Extract* of 1741; (c) Wesley's *Works*, VII.307-53, VIII.3-138 (1771), in which the asterisks appear, and whose text is here followed; and (d) beginning pages in this volume.

Sect.	1735 Ed.	1741 Ed.	Works (1772)	Page	Sect.	1735 Ed.	1741 Ed.	Works (1772)	Page
1	I:1.3	I:1.2	VII:310	21	54-55	I:22.1	I:16.4	VII:336	24
2	I:2.1	I:2.1	VII:310	21	56	I:22.5	I:16.5	VII:336	24
3	I:2.3	I:2.3	VII:311	21	57	I:23.1	I:17.1	VII:337	24
4	I:2.4	I:2.3	VII:311	21	58	I:23.2	I:17.2	VII:337	24
5	I:2.4	I:2.4	VII:312	21	59-61	I:23.4	I:17.4	VII:338	24
6-8	I:3.2	I:3.2	VII:313	21	62-63	I:23.5	I:17.5	VII:338	25
9	I:3.3	I:3.3	VII:313	21	64	I:23.7	I:17.7	VII:338	25
10-11	I:3.5	I:3.5	VII:314	21	65-66	I:23.9	I:17.8	VII:339	25
12-14	I:3.6	I:3.6	VII:314-5	21	67	I:24.3	I:18.2	VII:340	25
15	I:4.2	I:4.2	VII:315	21	68	I:25.2	I:19.1	VII:342	25
16-17	I:5.1	I:5.1	VII:316	22	69	I:25.6	I:19.4	VII:343	25
18-19	I:7.1	I:6.1	VII:317	22	70	II:1.2	II:1.2	VII:345	25
20	I:7.3	I:6.3	VII:317	22	71-72	II:1.3	II:1.3	VII:345	25
21-22	I:10.1	I:8.1	VII:319	22	73-75	II:1.4	II:1.4	VII:345-6	25-26
23	I:11.1	I:9.1	VII:320	22	76-77	II:1.5	II:1.5	VII:346	26
24	I:11.4	I:9.4	VII:320	22	78	II:1.6	II:1.6	VII:346	26
25	I:12.2	I:10.2	VII:321	22	79-80	II:1.7	II:1.7	VII:347	26
26	I:12.2	I:10.4	VII:322	22	81	II:1.8	II:1.8	VII:347	26
27	I:13.3	I:10.5	VII:322	22	82	II:2.2	II:2.2	VII:349	26
28	I:13.4	I:10.6	VII:322	22	83	II:3.1	II:3.1	VII:349	26
29-33	I:13.5	I:10.7	VII:323	22-23	84-85	II:3.3	II:3.3	VII:350	26
34-35	I:13.6	I:10.8	VII:323	23	86-89	II:4.1	II:4.1	VII:351	26
36-37	I:15.1	I:12.1	VII:326	23	90	II:4.2	II:4.2	VII:352	26
38	I:16.1	I:13.1	VII:327	23	91	II:5.2	II:5.2	VII:353	27
39-40	I:16.2	I:13.1	VII:327	23	92-95	II:5.3	II:5.3	VII:353	27
41-43	I:16.4	I:13.4	VII:328	23	96	II:6.2	II:6.2	VIII:4	27
44	I:19.1	I:14.4	VII:330	23	97	II:6.3	II:6.3	VIII:4	27
45	I:19.2	I:14.4	VII:330	23	98	II:6.4	II:6.4	VIII:5	27
46	I:19.4	I:14.5	VII:331	23	99-100	II:7.1	II:7.1	VIII:5	27
47-48	I:20.2	I:15.2	VII:331-2	24	101-2	II:7.2	II:7.2	VIII:5-6	27
49	I:20.3	I:15.3	VII:332	24	103	II:7.3	II:7.3	VIII:6	27
50-51	I:20.4	I:15.4	VII:332-3	24	104-5	II:7.1	II:7.1	VIII:6-7	27
52	I:20.8	I:15.7	VII:334	24	106	II:7.2	II:7.2	VIII:7	27
53	I:21.3	I:16.3	VII:336	24	107	II:8.3	II:8.3	VIII:7	27

Sect.	1735 Ed.	1741 Ed.	Works (1772)	Page
108-10	II:8.4	II:8.4	VIII:8	27-28
111	II:8.5	II:8.5	VIII:8	28
113-4	II:9.2	II:9.2	VIII:9	28
115-6	II:9.4	II:9.4	VIII:10	28
117	II:9.7	II:9.6	VIII:11	28
118	II:10.1	II:10.1	VIII:12	28
119	II:10.3	II:10.2	VIII:12	28
120	II:10.5	II:10.4	VIII:13	28
121-3	II:11.4	II:11.4	VIII:15	28
124	II:11.5	II:11.5	VIII:15	28
125	II:12.2	II:12.2	VIII:16	29
126-8	II:12.3	II:12.3	VIII:17	29
129-30	II:12.4	II:12.4	VIII:18	29
131	II:12.5	II:12.5	VIII:18	29
132	II:12.9	II:12.7	VIII:18	29
133	II:12.10	II:12.8	VIII:19	29
134	II:12.11	II:12.9	VIII:19	29
135-6	III:1.2	III:1.2	VIII:23	29-30
137-41	III:2.1	III:2.1	VIII:23-24	30
142-3	III:2.3	III:2.3	VIII:24-25	30
144	III:3.4	III:3.3	VIII:26	30
145-7	III:3.5	III:3.4	VIII:27	30
148	III:3.6	III:3.5	VIII:27	31
149-50	III:5.1	III:5.1	VIII:30	31
151	III:5.2	III:5.2	VIII:31	31
152-3	III:5.3	III:5.3	VIII:31	31
154-6	III:5.4	III:5.4	VIII:32	31
157-8	III:5.5	III:5.5	VIII:32	31
159-60	III:5.6	III:5.6	VIII:32-33	31-32
161-62	III:5.7	III:5.7	VIII:33	32
163	III:5.8	III:5.8	VIII:33	32
164-5	III:8.3	III:7.4	VIII:37	32
166	III:9.2	III:8.2	VIII:37	32
167-9	III:10.1	III:9.1	VIII:38-39	32
170	III:10.2	III:9.2	VIII:39	32
171-5	III:10.3	III:9.3	VIII:40	32-33
176-7	III:10.4	III:9.4	VIII:40	33
178-9	III:13.2	III:10.2	VIII:42	33
180-2	III:13.3	III:10.3	VIII:42	33
183	III:16.1	III:13.1	VIII:47	33
184	III:16.2	III:13.2	VIII:47	33
185	III:17.1	III:14.1	VIII:48	33
186	III:17.2	III:14.2	VIII:48	33
187	III:17.3	III:14.3	VIII:49	33
188-91	III:19.3	III:15.3	VIII:50	34
192	III:21.1	III:16.1	VIII:52	34
193	III:21.2	III:16.1	VIII:52	34
194	III:21.3	III:16.3	VIII:53	34
195	III:21.4	III:16.4	VIII:54	34
196	III:21.6	III:16.6	VIII:54	34
197	III:22.5	III:17.4	VIII:57	34
198-201	III:23.1	III:18.1	VIII:57	34-35
202-3	III:22.4	III:18.3	VIII:58-59	35
204-6	III:23.5	III:18.4	VIII:59	35
207	III:23.6	III:18.5	VIII:59	35
208	III:25.1	III:20.1	VIII:61	35
209	III:26.3	III:21.3	VIII:63	35
210-1	III:27.2	III:22.2	VIII:64	35
212	III:27.4	III:22.4	VIII:65	35-6
213	III:30.5	III:24.3	VIII:68	36
214	III:31.1	III:25.1	VIII:68	36
215	III:32.1	III:25.1	VIII:69	36
216	III:34.1	III:26.1	VIII:72	36
217-8	III:34.3	III:26.3	VIII:73	36
219	III:37.1	III:27.1	VIII:73	36
220	III:37.2	III:27.2	VIII:73	36
221-3	III:37.3	III:27.3	VIII:74	37
224	III:38.1	III:28.1	VIII:75	37
225	III:39.1	III:28.3	VIII:75	37
226-7	III:42.1	III:30.1	VIII:78-79	37
228-9	III:43.2	III:31.2	VIII:80	37
230	III:43.3	III:31.3	VIII:80	37
231	III:46.5	III:32.2	VIII:81	37
232-3	III:48.5	III:33.2	VIII:83	37
234	III:50.3	III:35.2	VIII:87	38
235	III:50.4	III:35.3	VIII:88	38
236	III:52.3	III:36.3	VIII:91	38
237-8	III:59.1	III:42.1	VIII:101-2	38
239	III:59.3	III:42.3	VIII:102	38
240-3	III:59.4	III:42.4	VIII:102-3	38
244-5	IV:1.2	IV:1.2	VIII:106	38
246-7	IV:1.3	IV:1.3	VIII:106	39
248	IV:1.4	IV:1.4	VIII:107	39
249	IV:2.1	IV:2.1	VIII:110	39
250	IV:2.5	IV:2.5	VIII:112	39
251	IV:2.6	IV:2.6	VIII:113	39
252-4	IV:3.1	IV:3.1	VIII:113-4	39
255	IV:3.2	IV:3.2	VIII:114	39
256	IV:3.4	IV:3.3	VIII:115	39
257-9	IV:4.1	IV:4.1	VIII:115-6	40
260	IV:4.2	IV:4.2	VIII:116	40
261	IV:7.2	IV:6.2	VIII:119	40
262	IV:8.1	IV:7.1	VIII:120	40
263	IV:12.2	IV:10.2	VIII:128	40
264	IV:14.2	IV:12.1	VIII:132	40
265-6	IV:15.1	IV:13.1	VIII:133	40
267	IV:15.2	IV:13.1	VIII:133	40
268	IV:16.1	IV:14.1	VIII:134	41

The Sources of Wesley's Selections
Pierre Poiret, *Instructions for Children*

Wesley's highlighting of passages from this work is so slight that it did not seem imperative to attempt to secure a copy of Poiret's *Principes* from England, one apparently not being available in the United States. Under the circumstances, it seemed sufficient to supply simply (a) the highlighted section numbers, (b) the corresponding section numbers in Wesley's version of Poiret by section, lesson, and paragraph, (c) the pages in Wesley's *Works*, Vol. XXIV (1773) containing the asterisked passages, where it is entitled "Instructions for Children," and (d) the page numbers of the current volume.

Sect.	1767 Ed.	Works (1773)	Page	Sect.	1767 Ed.	Works (1773)	Page
1	II:3.4	XXIV:131	47	8	III:6.11	XXIV:138	47
2	II:3.7	XXIV:131	47	9	III:7.5	XXIV:138	47
3	II:6.5	XXIV:132	47	10	III:9.12	XXIV:140	47
4	II:6.6	XXIV:133	47	11	III:10.2	XXIV:141	47
5	II:1.5	XXIV:133	47	12	III:9.12	XXIV:144	47
6	III:2.1	XXIV:134	47	13	III:3.3	XXIV:145	47
7	III:3.6	XXIV:135	47	14	III:5.1	XXIV:146	47

The Sources of Wesley's Selections
Saint-Cyran, *Christian Instructions*

Shown here after the section numbers are the corresponding details of sources: (a) Arnauld's selections from Saint-Cyran, first edition (1672), (b) Wesley's *Works*, Vol. XXIV (1773), where it is entitled "Christian Reflections," and (c) page numbers in the current volume.

Sect.	1672 Ed.	Works (1773)	Page	Sect.	1672 Ed.	Works (1773)	Page
1	3	1	55	13	111	29	56
2	16	5	55	14	136	34	56
3	20	7	55	15	170	41	56
4	31	11	55	16	174	42	56
5	36	12	55	17	181	43	57
6	37	13-14	55	18	183	44	57
7	41	14	55	19	190	47	57
8	61	17	55	20	218	58	57
9	68	18	55	21	242	66	57
10	75	19	56	22	287	72	57
11	83	20	56	23	312	77	57
12	84	21	56	24	332	82	57

Sect.	1672 Ed.	Works (1773)	Page	Sect.	1672 Ed.	Works (1773)	Page
25	338	84	57	65	750	214	64
26	376	99	57-58	66	752	216	64
27	397	104	58	67	756	217	64
28	433	111	58	68	759	218	64
29	435	112	58	69	779	224	65
30	465	119	58	70	692	227	65
31	466	467	58	71	793	228	65
32	467	121	58-59	72	802	234	65
33	469	122	59	73	813	238	65
34	468	123	59-60	74	822	241	65
35	472	125	60	75	832	243	65
36	477	126	60	76	836	249	65
37	479	128	60	77	852	253	66
38	482	129	60-61	78	861	254	66
39	494	130	61	79	872	256	66
40	535	151	61	80	885	264	66
41	553	157	61	81	895	267	66
42	568	159	61	82	899	269	66
43	588	162	61	83	921	272	66
44	627	169	61	84	924	274	66
45	628	170	61	85	926	276	66
46	631	171	61-62	86	932	280	66
47	634	173	62	87	952	285	66
48	639	174	62	88	984	301	67
49	645	178	62	89	986	302	67
50	650	179	62	90	1024	311	67
51	651	180	62	91	1025	312	67
52	660	182	62	92	1029	314	67
53	671	186	62	93	1040	315	67
54	676	188	63	94	1072	317	67
55	680	189	63	95	1077	318	68
56	692	192	63	96	1108	321	68
57	696	193	63	97	1112	322	68
58	710	199	63	98	1124	325	68
59	720	202	63	99	1128	326	68
60	727	204	63	100	1140	330	68
61	731	207	64	101	1153	331	68
62	739	208	64	102	1160	331	68
63	745	210	64	103	456	335	68-69
64	748	212	64	104	457	336	69

The Sources of Wesley's Selections
J. J. Duguet, *Letters on Morality and Piety*

Wesley made extracts from Duguet's first two letters only, the first under the title, "Instructions for Members of Religious Societies," the second, "Directions to Preserve Fervency of Spirit." He divided each into numbered sections. Here we show (a) these sections, preceded by "I" or "II" to indicate which of the letters was the source, (b) their corresponding numbers by part (in Letter I only) in Duguet's *Lettres* (Paris, 1708), (c) the corresponding sections in the full selection in Wesley's *Works*, Vol. XXIV (1773), and (d) the page numbers in the current volume.

Sect.	1708 Ed.	Works (1773)	Page	Sect.	1708 Ed.	Works (1773)	Page
I:[1]	III:1	I:1	77-78	II:1	1	II:1	82
I:1	III:4	I:2	78	II:2	3	II:2	82
I:2	II:7-8	I:4	78	II:3	11	II:6	82-83
I:3	III:9	I:5	78	II:4	13	II:7	83
I:4	III:9	I:6	78-79	II:5	14	II:8	83
I:5	III:12	I:7	79	II:6	15	II:9	83
I:6	III:15	I:10	79-80	II:7	20	II:10	83-84
I:7	III:16	I:11	80	II:8	21	II:11	84
I:8	III:19	I:13	80-81	II:9	22	II:12	84
I:9	IV:1	I:14	81	II:10	24	II:14	84
I:10	IV:4	I:15	81-82	II:11	26	II:16	84

INDEX